Cultural Practices and Identity Politics in Manipur

About the Centre

The *Centre for Alternative Discourse, Manipur,* which is run by Research Foundation Charitable Trust, a registered body, constituted under the Indian Trusts Act 1882, and registered under Registration of Societies Act 1908, publishes the journal *Alternative Perspectives* (ISSN 2248 –969X). The *Centre for Alternative Discourse, Manipur* is an outcome of year long discussion and consultation among the academicians, intellectuals, social activists and scholars of the State with a view to promote a sensible, systematic and informed study on various issues in human society through the publication of an academic journal. The very inception of the idea of establishing a centre to promote constructive, insightful, critical enquiries into the existing material conditions and circumstances in the State, the region and the world, which has a direct or indirect bearing upon the lives of the people came from recognition of a need to critique the economies, politics, history and culture of the realities surrounding our lives. The establishment of the *Centre for Alternative Discourse, Manipur* represents our understanding that we belong to a critical historical epoch.

About the Editors

Lisham Henthoiba is currently working on *Popular Movement in Manipur* for his doctoral thesis at Department of Political Science, Manipur University. The author is also a Senior Research Fellow, UGC. He is also associated with the quarterly journal *Alternative Perspectives* published by the Centre for Alternative Discourse, Manipur (CADM).

Laishram Churchil is a journalist by profession. He is presently working as Senior Sub-Editor of the Imphal based English daily paper, *The Sangai Express*. He is also associated with the quarterly journal *Alternative Perspectives* published by the Centre for Alternative Discourse, Manipur (CADM).

Cultural Practices
and
Identity Politics in Manipur

Edited by

Lisham Henthoiba
Laishram Churchil

Published for
Centre for Alternative Discourse, Manipur
by
CONCEPT PUBLISHING COMPANY PVT. LTD.
NEW DELHI-110059

ISBN-13: 978-93-5125-143-9

First Published 2015

Published and Printed by

Concept
Since 1974

Concept Publishing Company Pvt. Ltd.
A/15-16, Commercial Block, Mohan Garden
New Delhi-110059 (India)
T: 25351460, 25351794, *F*: 091-11-25357109
E: publishing@conceptpub.com, W: www.conceptpub.com
Editorial Office: H-13, Bali Nagar, New Delhi-110 015, India.

Cataloging in Publication Data--Courtesy: D.K. Agencies (P) Ltd. <docinfo@dkagencies.com>

Cultural practices and identity politics in Manipur / edited by Lisham Henthoiba, Laishram Churchil.
pages cm
Includes bibliographical references and index.
ISBN 9789351251439

1. Ethnicity--India--Manipur. 2. Identity politics--India--Manipur. 3. Political customs and rites--India--Manipur. 4. Manipur (India)--Economic conditions. I. Henthoiba, Lisham, editor. II. Churchil, Laishram, editor. III. Centre for Alternative Discourse, Manipur.issuing body.

DDC 305.80095417 23

Acknowledgements

The *Centre for Alternative Discourse, Manipur* (CADM) is extremely thankful to all the contributors who have translated their thoughts and researches into writings for *Alternative Perspectives,* a quarterly academic journal (ISSN 2248-969X) based in Imphal. The Centre is also grateful to the readers and well wishers, whose critiques and suggestions have immensely helped to arrive at constructive reviews, rethinking and exchange of ideas. Without the mention of the subscriber, individuals and institutions, this acknowledgement would be incomplete.

Like all social activity, academic exercise is also a collective endeavour. In the course of preparation for the publication of this book many individuals have assisted and contributed in varied degree and capacity. In this regard we are thankful particularly to Arambam Noni, Chongtham Gunamani, Hanjabam Isworchandra, Hidam Premananda, Konthoujam, Indrakumar, Laishram Krishna Chandra, Laishram Malemmagal, Laishram Nandalal, Moirangthem Prakash and R.K Smejita for their meticulous insight into the technical aspects and the series of discussions that took place on the framework of every essay. We are extremely grateful for their constructive suggestions without which the book would have been difficult to become a reality underscoring the diverseness of the theme that this volume deals.

We would like to take this opportunity to express our sincere gratitude and indebtedness to N. Homeshwar and O. Benimala for their priceless support and constant motivation to the young scholars at the CADM to think and reflect on the critical issues in the State and region (NE India). Nevertheless, their narration and reflections on the unrecorded accounts of contemporary events of Manipur have enriched all of us intellectually.

Last but not the least, we would like to extend our sincere thanks to Mr. A.K. Mittal and Concept Publishing Company Pvt. Ltd. (New Delhi) for the publication of present book on behalf of the CADM. It is true that without their support and encouragement the book may not have seen the light of the day. We are positively hoping and looking forward to more such encouragement from Concept Publishing Company in the years to come.

Contents

PART – III
UNDERSTANDING RESISTANCE

Profile of the Contributors

Diana Naorem is a doctoral fellow at the Centre for Political Studies, Jawaharlal Nehru University, New Delhi. The author can be reached at <dianachanu@gmail.com>.

Rekha Konsam is a doctoral fellow in the Department of Sociology, Delhi School of Economics (University of Delhi) Delhi. She can be reached at <rekhakonsam@gmail.com>.

Sonthang Haokip is Assistant Professor at the Department of History, Moirang College, Government of Manipur. He is also senior doctoral fellow in the Department of History, Manipur University. He took keen interest in the Kuki political movements. He can be reached at <sonthanghaokip@gmail.com>.

G. Amarjit Sharma received his doctoral degree from the Centre for Political Studies, Jawaharlal Nehru University, New Delhi. He is a faculty at The North-East Studies Research Centre, School of Social Science, Jawaharlal Nehru University, New Delhi. The author can be reached at <g.amarjit@gmail.com>.

K. Gyanendra Singh received his doctoral degree from Assam University, Silchar. He is Assistant Professor, Department of Economics, Indian Business School, Hyderabad. The author can be reached at <gyanendra_eco@yahoo.com>.

Malem Ningthouja has submitted his doctoral thesis to the Department of History, University of Delhi. He can be reached at <mningthouja@yahoo.com>.

Otojit Kshetrimayum received his doctoral degree from the Centre for Study of Social System, Jawaharlal Nehru University, New

Delhi. He is Associate Fellow, V.V. Giri National Labour Institute, Noida. He can be reached at <otojit@gmail.com>.

Shreema Ningombam teaches Political Science at Nambol L. Sanoi College, Nambol, Manipur. She can be reached at <shreema.ningombam@gmail.com>.

Shilleima Chanu Naoroibam is a doctoral scholar at the Centre for Historical Studies, Jawaharlal Nehru University, New Delhi. She is working on gender historiography in the context of the North East for her doctoral thesis. She can be reached at <shilleima7@gmail.com>.

Silvia Lisam received her doctoral degree from the Department of Economics, Manipur University. She is teaching Economics at G. P. Women College, Imphal, Manipur. She can be reached at <silvie.lisam@gmail.com>.

Introduction

The broad themes of this book grapple with three different but interrelated themes which mark three crucial elements of contemporary Manipur: the issues of economic backwardness, armed conflict and claims over identity. To begin with identity, one may note that the process of reclaiming identities is entangled with the question of political economy of community relations and it has generated violent turns in various instances. As much as peace is desired along the way, material conditions, however, have consequently produced another equally strong desire, one that justifies distancing away from other communities as well. This is why material conditions of identity discourse need to be seriously enquired upon. It is this condition, as we believe, that shape the politics of two possibilities of our times—that of bringing peace and breaking with a hegemonic notion of peace.

Every "imagined" nation and homeland (as they would say but not necessarily in the Andersonian sense) has been plying old ties and relationships, either by totally disowning or reinventing them in substantively different forms with inflection or depreciation, historical or political. The practice of such kind is always impinged on benefits, which such a political act would ensure. It uses subtle means and methods by rallying around cultural and ritual elements not only to achieve the desired goal but also to create a space for negotiating with the self and achieve a state of social homeostasis.

However, politics of identity as we have seen has also engaged with two undercurrents, which perhaps are contradictory but not certainly trapped in a duality in the sense of inability to resolve contradictions, whatsoever possible ways in which logic of contradiction operate in it. Politics of national, ethnic or tribal identity might hold ground *perhaps* because they levitate over historical bindings of the *ethne*, tribe or nation. But this cannot be generalised and applied to another politics of identity, which is not about claiming and recognition in terms of nationality or nation, *ethne* or tribe. One form of this politics (there are others, though) is the sexual politics of identity (involving gender issues and forms of assertion). Grounded in both critiquing and reinventing "traditionality", its value and morality as a site of exercising identity, the sexual politics also questions the tenets of modernity by intervening in how gender is constituted in the language of the dominant, patriarchy being one. Linking to the former, it claims, for example, that nationalist project of "liberation" does not take into account understanding of gender. In such an understanding, woman and motherhood are mere symbols, politically articulated in the nationalist imagination only to reinforce patriarchal values. And yet, there are other ways in which practicing the notion of alternative woman, such as *maibi*, in the very bastion of tradition seriously questions the patriarchy itself.

The first three articles deals with the seemingly contradictory understanding of identity as given above. In "Inside and Outside of Ethnic Enclosures: Khoibu as a *Separate* Tribe", G. Amarjit Sharma looks into how tribe in Manipur as both a notion and identity have evolved not merely as a stage of social formation but largely as a response to other social and political formations in a geographical space called valley. Taking Khoibu tribe as a case in point, he argues that tribal identity is porous suggesting the deeper political experience where it comes into negotiation with "others", which happen to be, in most of the cases, dominant ethnic identities.

In the second essay "The Political Interpretation of Ritual: The Case of *Lai Haraoba* of Manipur", Otojit Kshetrimayum tries to locate the resurgence of *Lai Haraoba* within the contour of identity politics in Manipur in recent times. *Lai Haraoba* is invoked as part of a cultural project to reassert and reconstruct an integral "Manipuri identity" of the pre-Hindu period. Otojit, while focusing on the political practice of rituals, however, argues that the revival of *Lai Haraoba* has less to do with "old Meitei custom".

In the next essay, "*Lai Haraoba* and Role of the *Maibis*", Shilleima Chanu Naoroibam examines the institution of *maibi* in *Lai*

Haraoba in order to understand gender practice, which according to her, is central to the ritual. *Lai Haraoba*, other than being a festival, is also a cultural theatre of contestation against patriarchal power and ideology. This is possible, she argues, through the ritual being a site where sexual harmony of two contrasting images of woman—ideal domesticated woman and alternative lifestyle as *maibi*—is achieved and performed.

The second theme of this book is on economic situation of the State. A deeper reading of the essays in totality reveals the chaotic situation of Manipur. Identity politics is about liberation from a perceived form of repression and exploitation. The liberation would be complete only when material well-being is also taken into account. Present chaotic economic reality of Manipur and the North-East is captured by four articles.

In the essay, "Economic Question in Manipur and Discourse of Development", Malem Ningthouja argues that economic crisis in Manipur emanates from Manipur's unfavourable balance of exchange with the Indian capitalist economy. The crisis has its historical root to Manipur's merger with the Dominion of India in 1949. As a result, he argues, the unfolding of the crisis is the most decisive character of Manipur's relation to the capitalist economy of India.

In the following essay, "Perspective on the Industrial Scenario in Manipur", K. Gyanendra Singh shows that backwardness of the industrial sector in Manipur is the result of various factors, for example, non-availability of core natural resources, geographical isolation leading to high transport cost, topography, paucity of infrastructural facilities, limited size of the local market. However, as he argues, establishment of industries having strong dyadic linkage with available local resources will help in sustaining industries in the long run for a land-locked State like Manipur. In this context, agriculture and horticulture, he argues, will boost industrialization while handloom, handicrafts, cane and bamboo based industries should run next in priority.

"Employment Structure of Agricultural Labourers in Manipur" is another essay where Silvia Lisam explores labour process in agricultural activities of two selected rural population in the villages of Taobungkhok and Tejpur. By comparing the two villages, she argues that locational as well as occupational distance from urban centre is one among other decisive factors contributing to employment structures in agricultural activities of rural population. On the whole, the findings of the field investigation show that agricultural labourers in both the villages under study rely on multiple occupations, as the employment potential in each occupation is limited and seasonal.

Finally the last theme dwell into the issues that has affected without exclusiveness of any individual who lived or travelled in this part of the world, i.e., the issue of resistance. "Protest" as an act of resistance or expression of denial through various modes has been a continuing feature of Manipur. Protest is not a uniform and singular event. If one looks into the ways in which protests are practiced and articulated in Manipur in the recent past, there is no doubt to say that protest creates a language and through protest the practitioners' world is put into a field of meaning and interpretation. How then do we have to understand protest from the point of view of the practitioners? How are multiple forms of protest coalesced, organised and displayed within the field of meanings they produced or rather created?

In this context, one of the concerns of this theme would be to displace the centrality of the given meanings of the ideas of justice and democracy which are occasioned particularly in liberal theorization and many of its transformations including neoliberal vicissitudes. The purpose is to chart limits of that which the given order of formal and constitutional archives produces as meanings, values and norms. The protests on various issues which people expressed often evoke questions. For instance the question such as, will it be possible for us to think of the notions of 'rights', 'justice' and 'democracy' in terms of these being constant creations through an engagement with the hegemonic formations including the state institutions and those operating outside of it? It will enable us to explore any possible dialogue, contradiction and contestation between formal and constitutional archives and practices on one hand and creations of justice, rights and democracy that are produced by protest politics in Manipur in the last few decades or so, on the other.

We hope to draw on the diversity of experiences of dissent and protest, the practitioners' worldview in their engagement with "counter-hegemony" in order to map protest practices of students, *Meira Paibis*, civil and political right groups, subaltern resistance especially to Loktak and many other hydro-electric projects being taken up in Manipur and North-East region, etc. To add to this is the practice of political violence and the ways in which it evokes a wider implication of a particular form of politics which is constituted on the question of life and death. In order to see the diverse effect on everydayness of fear and repression, the following essays also seek to open up a critical rendering of the dominant sensibility of "national security" as practiced in Manipur in particular and North-East in general. This section consists of four articles on varied protest movement ranging from non-homogenised power formation in a seemingly non- patriarchal society to the resistance of motherhood against varied forms of atrocities and resistance being practiced at the cultural site.

Through a feminist reading of some of the common practices in Manipur society, particularly among the Meiteis, Shreema Ningombam argues in "Mapping Repressive Practices against Women in the Meitei Society" that the perceived high social status of the women does not escape from underlying repression of women. The subordination of women takes a worse form through their being constructed as political-ideological figure, *Ima*. Addressing this issue she maintains that the nationalist question in Manipur cannot be addressed without taking into account the questions of gender.

Naorem Diana's article entitled "Motherhood and the Politics of Resistance" focuses on the centrality of Women's movement particularly expressed in the form of *Meira Paibis,* literally means torch bearer and its historicity. One of the central or crux areas of the study is the concept of motherhood, which in her view goes much beyond mere giving birth to children. As she feels motherhood goes much beyond this, and includes those women, who despite having missed the reproduction process, become mothers by performing the latter part, i.e., by bringing up the child, helping him or her take shape. In the meantime, various scientific advancements have expanded the conventional definition of motherhood, stressing it out to include other avenues of reproduction, involving more players and stakeholders. Consequently, debates surrounding the notion of motherhood became more complex, making any response to the question—who is a mother—a contested one. Her article critically look at the 'power' aspect of motherhood and their role as protector and defender of their children and people in a conflict ridden Manipur.

Article beautifully traces evolution of women's protest and struggle from the *Nisha Bandi* to *Meira Paibis*. The transformation of women collective struggle from *Nisha Bandi* to *Meira Paibis* also represents a crucial shift in the socio-political experiences of the people of Manipur. The crucial period of the 80s of the twentieth century show the growth and birth of armed struggle. It attempts to explore how motherhood as a trope and practice becomes a rallying principle, which had led to the various form of human rights violation such as forced disappearances, rape, extra-judicial killings, under the so called policy of counter insurgency operations by the State law enforcing agency. The article also tries to explore the case, where 'motherhood' has gained a degree of success in mobilising specific struggles.

The next article entitled "Resisting the 'Other': Ethnographic Exploration of the *Lai Haraoba* in the Contemporary" by Rekha Konsam deals with the revival of *Lai Haraoba* in the Meitei settlement area of Manipur and concerted effort of the people to focus attention to the festival at the level of practice. This resurgence or revival of the festival of *Lai Haraoba* can be seen as an articulation of the Meitei cultural identity by juxtaposing Meitei self with that of Hinduism as 'other'. Konsam article attempts to focus on the articulation of a self-conscious Meitei cultural identity. In this articulation, it is not so much a question of what constitutes it but, significantly, what does *not* constitute it. In her view *Lai Haraoba* has emerged as a cultural space in which resistance against an overarching Hindu cultural influence which comes to constitute cultural 'other' is predominantly visible. The chapter explores this space as a self-conscious space for the articulation of a Meitei cultural identity. In her chapter the author acknowledges the *Lai Haraoba* challenges that *Lai Haraoba* as a subject of enquiry poses to any researcher. Her present exploration of the festival is limited as it seeks to address only certain aspects with particular focus being given on the aspect of cultural identity articulated by the practitioners.

The article titled "Kuki National Assembly: Historicity and Evolution" by Sonthang Haokip seeks to trace the growth of political consciousness among the Kukis with the coming of British into the present day North-Eastern region of India. It also discusses how the foremost organization among the Kukis—the Kuki National Assembly (KNA) acted as a torchbearer as far as the history of Kuki National

Movement is concerned. It deals with the Kuki National Assembly as a platform working for the Kuki interest at large and not as a Political Party as such. This chapter elaborately deals with the evolution of Kuki political movements with particular focus being given on the birth and evolution of Kuki National Assembly (KNA). The article analyses the Kukis' political movement (relating to the Kukis of Manipur) into two phases; (1) KNA Period (1946–1980); and (2) Post-KNA Periods, from 1980s onwards. One of the central arguments in the article is the transformation of initially non-violent movement into armed/violent movement as a result of the continuous ignorance of the State and Central government. In the final part the article deals with events in the post-KNA phase with particular emphasis on the suspension of Operation (SoO), a tripartite agreement the Kuki armed insurgent groups on the one hand and Manipur State government and Government of India on the other hand.

Lisham Henthoiba
Laishram Churchil

Part – I
Identity Assertion and Cultural Practices

1

Inside and Outside of Ethnic Enclosures

Khoibu as a Separate Tribe

G. Amarjit Sharma

Much of what we know today as tribe is not what earlier anthropologists understood as a particular type of society and a stage of social evolution. For tribe is no more an isolated, self-contained and primitive social formation. It is also increasingly difficult to define. The problem of a clear definition on tribe assumes a chronic form in South Asia, where tribes had co-existed with other types of social formation for centuries (Beteille 1998, 187). What we know as the Scheduled Tribe (ST) in India has not only been vaguely defined, but also avoids the issue of formal definition; it merely stands for a set of communities listed in an official schedule (Beteille 1998, 188). Beyond such official enumeration, tribe is both constituted by and constitutive of the social, political and geographical factors in a place. If one looks in North-East India and broader Indo-Myanmar areas, tribe gets defined during various encounters with valley society and polity; encounters had/have occurred both within the colonial and post-colonial states. F. K. Lehman (1963) argued that the social system in the Chin Hills in Myanmar was moulded in response to the valley Burman.

In similar sense, tribes in Manipur have been shaped as a result of various encounters with valley society. For instance, tribe as a society moulded through rejection of any affinities with other social formation is seen in the ways Naga society has been constructing with respect to the valley Meitei society in Manipur (Sharma 2007).

Hence, in hill areas of North-East India, tribe has been evolved not merely as a stage of social formation or merely as a society intimately associated with other social formations, but largely as a response to other social and political formations in a geographical space called valley. Hills have become a label that represents the life-worlds of tribe. The response, further, led to fusion of tribes into generic ethnic identities. This process encloses one group of tribes from another, such as the Naga and Kuki/Kuki-Chin-Mizo tribes. Yet, tribes are porous and for many of the smaller tribes, articulating tribal identity both outside and inside such enclosures has been their survival strategy.

We focus broadly on the social analysis of relationships among and within tribes in hill areas of Manipur. Not all the tribes are listed in the State's ST list and in our context official tribes refer to those tribes listed in the State's list of ST. The State of Manipur has so far enumerated 33 Scheduled Tribes. But the study is a case of a 'sub-tribe' of an official tribe demanding the status of ST. We select the case of the Khoibus living in south-eastern hill region of Manipur, who are included under the officially listed tribe named as the Maring. However, the Khoibus claim to be a separate tribe, which the larger sections of Maring tribe deny. However, what appears after close study is that this is not a situation strictly internal to a tribe, but the equation of powers among the ethnic enclosures in hill areas of the State also matters while deciding who should be recognised as tribe or ST. Even the State that has the authority to recognise tribes as Schedule Tribe is influenced by strong lobby of a powerful tribe who is against the recognition of certain groups as ST.

The case study of Khoibus is important because it is a case of negotiating a distinct tribal identity in between the ethnic enclosures in Manipur. It is argued that the enclosures of tribes around the generic ethnic identities like Naga have made cultural identity of Khoibus invisible. The study is also important in the sense that despite non-recognition of Khoibu as an official tribe, they live themselves as an independent tribe. The Khoibu, if one asks their identity, will not identify as Maring or part of Maring, but as Khoibu. We argue that Khoibu's sense of tribe, though based on their discovery of social and cultural history and looks like an isolated social phenomenon, itself is the product of their response to official consideration of them as sub-group of Maring tribe, social imposition on them as part of Maring social structure and ethnic imposition to them as Naga. Social history is the product of such response.

While looking at this, the Khangshim village has been identified as site of enquiry. In our context, this village is more than a mere social unit; rather it is the site of negotiation for surviving as independent tribe. The Khangshim village is a peculiar case especially because the foothill in which it is located has increasingly become a non-significant space between the "hills" and "valley" around which the ethnic politics in the region are revolved. Perhaps, the case of Khoibus at the foothill area has given a different story as far as the politics of identity in the region is concerned.

Invisibility of Khoibus

The Khoibus are settled in hills and foothills of the south-east Manipur. One of their settlement areas is the Khangshim village at a foothill. The village is apparently separated from other settlement areas of the Marings. It is also a neighbouring village to a largely Meitei populated place called Kakching (a town in Thoubal district). Many of the Khoibus in the hills and foothill areas have been migrated to urban areas of Imphal, the capital of Manipur, for reasons ranging from education, jobs to other economic activities. Those villages in hills are known to them as the ancestral villages, where there is a communal ownership of land.

Their first migration within the State appears to be the foothill areas, where there are local markets such as Pallel and Kakching bazaars. They are dependent on these markets both to sell their own products (handloom products are popular) and to buy daily needs. Khoibus maintain regular relationship with their ancestral villages at the Khoibu Khunjao (Khullen) in the hills. It is apparent from interaction with the Khoibus that Khangshim village is more like a satellite village of the Khoibu Khunjao. Khangshim is one of such satellite villages. The relationship between ancestral and satellite villages is political, for every group of people desires to be rooted in their ancestral land to prove their indigeneity. They have been in the local news in recent times because of their assertion as a different tribe from their official parent tribe Maring, and violent reactions from the Marings who oppose the demand. The Khalling clan of Khoibus bought the land where Khangshim village is located from the neighbouring Meiteis. The Khalling clan became and is still the head clan of the village as per their customarily laws.

The Khoibus are invisible (non-recognition of cultural identity) group of people amidst the ethnic enclosures. One does not find the name of Khoibu (as tribe) in unofficial listing of tribes. The unofficial list of tribes compiled by the United Naga Council Working Group (UNCWG) includes Maring as one of the constituent Naga tribes in Manipur and Nagaland. To the Khoibus compulsion to be recognised first as Maring and then as Naga is a paramount reality. This reality restricts the Khoibus from asserting their identity independently of the Naga nationalism. Largely, tribes in Manipur have been aggregated into major ethnic enclosures such as the Naga and Kuki/Kuki-Chin-Mizo. The collectivizing of tribes as either Naga or Kuki is something that the State (colonial and post-colonial States) and recently, ethnic civil society groups have engineered. Once the State engineered ethnic identity, it is the turn of the civil society that makes efforts to internalise that identity for different interests.

Prior to the listing of tribes into Scheduled Tribes in 1956, the State classified tribes into "any Naga tribe", "any Kuki tribe" and "any Lushai tribe". This had led to consolidation of tribes into these categories, and counter-emergence of other tribal identities, especially of those who did not like the name Kuki (anti-Thadou tribes). Despite the beginning of official listing, tribes in daily life have been survived as ethnic groups: Naga and Kuki/Kuki-Chin-Mizo. The post-independence movement (particularly in 1970 and after) for integrating Nagas in North-East India further solidified enclosures of tribes as the Naga tribes. Equally there have been the Kuki-Chin-Mizo tribes. The two groupings even had ethnic conflicts in 1990s. The Naga enclosure under its armed wing National Socialist Council of Nagaland—Issac-Muivah have imagined the "Naga inhabited hills districts" in Manipur, which shrinks the Kukis' space for political manoeuvres. However, against such seemingly naturalised ethnic boundaries, the description given to certain tribes as "culturally Kuki and politically Naga" is pretty confusing. Tribes like Anal, Moyons, Monsang, Marings, etc., are considered as culturally "Old Kukis", becoming "politically" Nagas in recent past. As a result, one needs to distinguish "cultural" and "political". Robbin Burhling (quoted in Barauh 2010, 249) argues that Naga is a political project and it is not a linguistic label. There is no linguistic unity among so called Naga tribes. Further, he comments that some groups whose language a linguist would classify as "Kuki" have declared themselves as Nagas. This shows that even the culturally diverse groups could become part of political Naga. One thing is clear, the ethnic enclosures are political in the sense that diverse tribal social structures, local beliefs, languages, etc., hardly create problem in falling under broader identity. For such identity has been propelled by the invention of greater, other ethnic group.

Within this political Naga, the need for ethno-nationalism has been so overwhelmed that there has been cultural construction of unity above all linguistic barriers. The first "Convention of the Naga people of Manipur" was held at Mao on May 16, 1970. It was resolved in the Convention:

> The Naga people aspiration to live together under a singular State has undoubtedly been motivated by a genuine patriotic urge. Moreover it is based on concrete and unchallenged facts such as that all the Naga inhabited areas in Manipur, Nagaland, NEFA and Assam are contiguous to each other and constitute a compact area, that the Nagas racially, socially, culturally and in all aspects of life are the same, that wherever they are and under whatever administrative set-up they may come, the sense of oneness among them remain ever strong and that into Nagaland State will be fulfilment of the common political aspiration (Resolution of 'The Naga People of Manipur' cited in, *Why Not South Nagaland* by the Forgotten Nagas (unpublished)).

The political Naga has used religion as an important instrument of transformation from culturally diverse tribes to a religious unit, "Nagaland for Christ". To Richard Eaton (1997), the pace of Christian conversion among the Nagas after independence was faster than before. In a changing world of Nagas when they have felt the need for political support across villages and States in the cause of Naga nationalism, Christ became a "high God". In the process, the Khoibu's official parent tribe, Maring became largely the Christian Naga. Rajat Kanti Das (1985, 1990) remarked that Marings were motivated to call themselves as Naga more by the church leaders than any other agency. Khoibus are learned to be largely Christians; though simultaneously old traditions still continue. And for them, Naga is a chosen political nomenclature. This choice, however, is one the smaller tribal groups are compelled to do, rather than a genuine decision.

For Khoibus, despite their historical fact of linkages genealogically to Haka, Falam, and Tedim Chins of Myanmar, they appear unwilling to remember and emphasise these links. Influence of Naga nationalism has been the crucial determining factor. The areas where the Khoibus inhabit are geographically contiguous with the Tangkhul in northern side of the Chandel district (Ukhrul district of Manipur). This geographical affinity made easy to influence Khoibus, among other neighbouring tribes to become Nagas. The present author was told that they became Naga through the spread of Christianity by the Tangkhul pastors.

Limits of Social Landscape

The Maring, one of the scheduled tribes in Manipur has four major sub-groups: Khoibu, Saibu, Kholleiya and Dak Thlanga. Among these groups, the Khoibus are the first one who have been asserting as a separate tribe. The present author was told that next to them, it is the turn of Saibu to assert as a different tribe. Though the Khoibus are officially considered as a sub-group of Maring, they consider themselves as having separate oral history, social structure and identity; they desire their "social facts" of having distinctive history and society are sufficed for recognizing them as a Scheduled Tribe under the Constitution of India. In fact, the then (office of the) Dewan of Manipur State (before it was merged to India in 1949) in its letter (dated 6th June 1949) had recognised the Khoibu as an independent tribe. However, the Government of India, in its Amendment to the Constitution (Scheduled Castes and Scheduled Tribes List Modification Order 1956), had dropped Khoibu from the list of Scheduled Tribes. The Khoibus Union, which represents the voice of the Khoibus, feels that the sole reason for non-recognition of Khoibu as Scheduled Tribe is because of the numerically larger fellow Marings, which has influenced the State government. The members of Khoibu Union (an organization established by Khoibus that works for their interests) contended that the State Assembly had passed resolution two times in favour of Khoibu as separate tribe. However, the State has not been able to move forward for a constitutional inclusion of them as the Scheduled Tribe. The numerical preponderance of fellow Marings has led to the political fact that Tengnoupal assembly constituency, which is their electoral constituency, has in most of the times elect a Maring candidate as Member of Legislative Assembly. Some Khoibus whom the present author met during fieldworks expressed helplessness of using electoral representation as a means for pushing forward their demand for inclusion as Scheduled Tribe because of less number in the State assembly constituency compared to their fellow Marings.

The so called Maring, from the perspective of the Khoibus, mostly are scattered in Machi and Tengnoupal Blocks of Chandel district of Manipur. Other villages of the Maring are also found dwelling in Chandel town and Chakpikarong subdivision of the same district, and also in Senapati and Ukhrul districts of Manipur. The spatial enclosure between the Khoibus, settled at Khangshim village and their ancestral village, Khoibu Khullen in the interior hills, on the one hand and the Maring particularly in the Machi and Tengnoupal Blocks, on the other, is a result of violent conflicts between the Maring and Khoibus, because of latter's assertion as a separate tribe. A Khoibu resident at Khangshim village, whom the author encountered at the first entry to the village, spoke on how the Maring youths came and destroyed the village. The Marings, to him, regularly monitor the meanings and manners of organisation of their public activities, such as community festival or village meetings, *etc*., in the Khoibu village. Before author's fieldwork in Khoibu village started, many stories were heard from the neighbouring Meiteis as well about how they were subjected to furies of the Maring youths for asserting themselves as separate tribe. When asked the neighbouring people about the Khoibus, their understanding was that of the Khoibus who had been displaced from Maring settlement areas. One distinct feature of the local perception of Khoibus of this village is that there was a clear identification of the Khoibus as the "rebellious" group from "mother" tribe Maring. This local perception strengthens, though unconsciously, the construction of Khoibus as a rebellious internel other. Stories about Khoibus being tortured and victimised at the hands of the majority tribal neighbour marked the author's first encounter.

Documenting Own History

A normal observer of the Khangshim village of about three thousand Khoibu residents, violently attacked by the so called Marings (to the Khoibus), may wonder as to how they preserve their history. A distinctive characteristic of the Khoibus is the documentation of their oral history in an inequal social order. Documenting one's own history has a specific cause. History, here, is a mode of asserting identity of a minor tribal group. This task was engineered by the Khoibu Union. The Union has written a document named as *Historical Background of Khoibu Tribe* for circulating among their people. The head office of the Union is located at the ancestral village (the Khoibu Khullen) and it has been considered among Khoibus as the representative body of their interests. Khoibus while asserting distinctive identity have evolved such a body as their agent to write their social history. There is a semantic shift in the assertion of Khoibu identity—the shift from the Maring-Khoibu tribe to Khoibu tribe and from a "sub-group" to an "independent tribe". Khoibus feel their identity has been misunderstood. This is well manifested in the document written by the Khoibu Union:

> Khoibu people are immediate neighbour to Maring people in terms of habitation. As such there is frequent social interaction between the *two tribes*. Religious fellowship, social activities like games and sports, etc., are jointly organised. There are inter-marriages between the two tribes. However, the *lingua franca* between the two tribes is the *Meiteilon* (Manipuri). By this reason or the other the Khoibu people are often called Khoibu Maring (italics added).

The Union has registered distinctiveness of the Khoibu as a tribe. It asserts, 'Khoibu is a tribe having its own distinctive culture, custom, language, genealogy, origin myth, migration, settlement, and the socio-political and religious organization. Khoibu people have Christian hymns and *Bible* written/translated in their own dialect'. The Khoibu as a tribe is proven through their defined social characteristics. Such characteristics are defined in the above mentioned document as follows:

> The Khoibu tribe bears some distinct characteristics such as head hunting, common dormitory for both male and female youth termed as *Yakhang* in the Khoibu dialect, socio-political system in the village level/village republic, a large quadrangular and hexagonal shield use in war or battlefield, settlement on the high lands, a crude form of agriculture practice for livelihood, every Khoibu village has a well-defined territory, population and independent internal and external policy exercised by the chief, assisted by the village council consisted of different clans, and common land ownership.

The Union traces genealogy of the Khoibus in myths which were believed to be the gifts of their ancestors. The English version of their myth of origin is given as follows:

Once we human beings were
Mangsawr *ruled*
Khayir *bound*
Mangsawr *was the male*
Khayir *was the female*
It was under the stone
It was beneath the earth
There, beneath the earth
There, under the stone
Neither was healthy
Nor was wealthy
To come onto the earth
To see the earth
There was gate of stones
Hard to open
Harder to open

The buffalo opened the hard gate
The buffalo opened the harder gate.

Despite the social fact of many tribes that they trace their origin from caves; the above origin myth signifies how the present Khoibu relates with the past. Khoibus do not relate with their past simply because there is or can be a past. A more serious reason is that they attempt to locate themselves within the "dislocated world"—dislocation for Khoibu could mean the unequal social condition that does not allow to name on their own terms, and establish an identity for them. The past is being invented through social history of migration. The origin of their migration is being traced in the Indo-Myanmar border. The English version of their migration myth is as follows:

Towards Mangrengphai we travelled
At Mangrengphai
Neither we were human
Nor were we fishes
For it was like a dream
It was called Mongrengphai
At Mongrengphai
Started learning to live
Learnt to prosper.

To their migration history, the Khoibus were said to have experienced their best and prosperous life under the reign of Mikhongpa in the Inthee Basin, Angoching Range and Yoomadung Hills, in the present Indo-Myanmar border. However, tragedy started when the Awa (the Burmese army) invaded their settlement areas. This led to their migration to settlement areas of the Marings. This in fact is telling how originally they were separated from the Maring and they became part of the Maring society by chance. But their memory of suffering at the hands of Burmese army has present relevance. A Khoibu resident at the Khangshim village had revealed that the Khoibus recall their memory of suffering under the Burmese armies because of the similar suffering at the hands of the Marings. It is their experience with the Maring that led the Khoibus to recall lives under the Burmese rule and how they migrated to the present settlement. In defining themselves as Khoibu, the Khoibus register the problematic side of the ways in which Maring tribe is representing them. In this act of defining, there is an attempt to give a message that they stand at par with the rest as an independent tribe, not as a constituent member of the Maring tribe. It is claimed that they have all the basic characteristics to be called as a tribe. The characteristics like 'head hunting, dormitory system, settlement on the high lands, village chief, village council, etc.', are in fact in common with other tribes as well. However, they seek to cut off the continuity with the rest by asserting the difference or asserting 'its own distinctive culture, custom, language, genealogy, history of origin, migration, settlement, socio-political and religious organization'. Hence, the affinities with, and distinctiveness of the Khoibus from their neighbouring tribal communities are asserted simultaneously.

This context of Khoibus reminds a theory of the modern representational democracy that 'subjects may have overthrowned the past and its spectres of ordained or divine hierarchy, but subjects only truly enter the present when they become self-representing. Further, in speaking for themselves, subjects move from a domain of exploitation, illusion and heteronomy to a spontaneous order of equal and self-determining individuals' (Colebrook 2005, 5). But the problem with this formulation, in the context of the present study is that the Khoibu as a subject have not forgotten their past nor overthrown their past. Instead, Khoibu as a subject is very much determined by his or her own past and cultural practices. In this way, Khoibu as an alienated self, if go by the above statement of the modern theory of representational democracy, is rescued by taking it as a constitutive part of the larger cultural context. The task of writing history by the Khoibus has been to define this cultural context. But the above theory of representation shares one important feature: entering the present reality as an equal subject and self-determining individuals. Again, the reality that Khoibu as a subject entered is a reality where he has to constantly negotiate for his culture and identity.

An interview with one of the respondents in the Khangshim village had revealed that they were not allowed to call as Khoibu. This respondent was severely beaten up for identifying as Khoibu when a group of Marings came to see him. Khoibu Union explains how the term Khoibu came to their lives and how they would like to be called:

> As our forefathers have been handing down our accounts orally from generation to generation; we called ourselves *Uipo*. The term *Khoi-pu* is derived from the version of *Khoi* which means bee and *Pu* is derived from *Akapu* which means owner. Therefore, Khoibu means the people who own bee, beehives, and honey in the indigenous land of Khoibu territory.... Though we called ourselves *Uipo*, we officially represent as Khoibu to avoid any confusion of our identity.

That the Khoibu as a subject has to constantly negotiate his own history and identity is borne by the immediate reality where the Maring still claims that the Khoibu is the constituent part of it. The active role of agency that the Khoibu Union has played by writing Khoibu's own history is also manifested in its ability to create crisis within the Maring society. A controversy was created within the Maring Student Union when the Khoibu represented as a separate unit to the Naga Student Union Delhi and submitted historical facts about the Khoibu to Naga Student Union Delhi and Naga Student Federation (NSF). The convener of the Maring Marnorap Delhi argues: "That, it was absolutely a matter of surprise and disappointment to all the Maring people when some of our dear brothers and sisters claiming themselves as Khoibu students, had raised, without any prior information to the authorities concerned, as an issue of affiliating themselves to NSUD (Naga Student Union Delhi) and as a separate Khoibu Unit apart from Maring Marnorap Delhi (MMD). If such demand is granted without prior consultation with the apex bodies of Maring, *viz.*, Maring Uparup Assembly (MUA), Maring Literature Society (MLS) and Maring Students' Union (MSU), it would lead to the provocation of misunderstandings and social unrest amongst the Marings regarding the history of Maring identities—social, cultural, literature, etc., ... On this account, the letters and historical facts about Khoibu submitted to NSUD and NSF, should be first and foremost referred and approved by the MUA, MLS and MSU" (the information is cited in the *Souvenir* of the Maring Student Union, 2004).

Now, it can be read that there are two levels of negotiation:

criticising the Maring identity as an imposed identity on the Khoibus; and the construction of Khoibu identity through its own written history. Yet the act of essentialising is similarly occurred in the case of Khoibus. They also emphasise the essence of being a Khoibu that the Khoibu has certain shared identity among them. However, the act of essentialising has different purposes for Maring and Khoibu. For the former, it wants to retain Khoibu as Maring tribe to resist any change in the dominant social order. But for the latter, it is an act of resisting this order. Thus, as far as Khoibu is concerned, it is worth mentioning that where a particular category of identity has been repressed, delegitimised or devalued in dominant discourses, a vital response may be to claim value for all those labelled by that category, thus implicitly invoking it in an essentialist way (Calhoun 1998, 17).

Nevertheless, the popular domain does not guarantee equal relationship among the ethnic groups. Interviews with the Khoibu residents revealed that the decision of the Khoibus to seek affiliation or belongingness to the larger Naga identity or seek cultural affinity with the neighbouring tribes is not measured by how much it shares with others in terms of cultural belief systems. Rather, it is decided by how much it can be secured by being in some relationships. This is supported by the perspective of ethnic group as organizational type, given by Fredrik Barth. Barth says that there is no simple one to one relationship between ethnic units and cultural similarities and differences. The features that are taken into account are not the sum of objective differences (or similarities), but only those which the actors themselves regards as significant. Hence, the basic orientation of any group is determined by the social effectiveness of those orientations (Barth 1969). The emphasis or reinforcement on cultural similarities is only the result of that strategy to give security to its own people. The possibility of having good relationship with the Meiteis is, however, dampened by the divide between the tribes and non-tribes. Such divide continues even after efforts of the Meitei civil society organizations to bridge the gap between the hill tribes and valley non-tribal population. Khoibus might have problems with the Maring tribe or other bigger tribes, but they feel that in the existing politics of the region their security lies in affiliating culturally and politically with a larger tribe.

The myth of cave origin, and its (myth) inclusion in the history writing of the Khoibus has in fact served this purpose. The Khoibus feel that they are culturally close to the neighbouring tribes like Anal, Mayon, Monsang and Lamkang who also have the myths of cave origin. For instance, Anals have the myth of cave origin. Anals' ancestors were believed to emerge from *Khul* or cave. The ancestors were Hanshu and Hantha. It is said that a tiger killed anyone who came out of this cave. Later the ancestors befriended a bird that they promised free feeding in the fields in return for their helps. The birds divert the attention of the tiger. In the mean time, they escaped from the cave. The myths of cave origin also found among the neighbouring tribes like Mayon and Monsang (Kabui 1985; Directorate for Development of Tribals and Backward Classes 1981).

What is intended to derive from this reference is that by making myth as a part of social history, the Khoibus make a strategy to ascertain cultural affinities with the rest of neighbouring tribes, yet they do not fail to emphasise their distinct identity. It can be further interpreted that though Khoibus need separate identity, ultimately the security of the smaller tribes lays in its affinity with the other neighbouring tribes or bigger tribes. This affinity is established through a skilfully worked out cultural similarities with the other tribes. It is in this project that the myth of cave origin serves a useful purpose. Fieldwork in the Khoibu village revealed that despite the fact that Khoibu shares cultural similarities with the Meiteis, the Khoibus still feel the needs for belongingness to larger Naga identity. But sometimes these needs are not out of one's choice rather by compulsion. But it should be mentioned that not all cultural elements are emphasised in these similarities. They also feel urgent to emphasise the distinctive identity of the Khoibus. Fredrik Barth argues that cultural difference could still persist despite inter-ethnic contact and interdependence (see Barth 1969).

Conclusion

The present study suggests that the assertion of the Khoibu identity from the Maring tribe is not merely a case of conflict between the two. The case study of history writing by the Khoibus is not merely a case of constructing identity through history. Exploring history writing by the Khoibu Union is a case of how the Khoibus articulate their identity *vis-à-vis* other larger ethnic communities. The case of Khoibus and their struggle to assert identity as a tribe is important because on different occasions they feel that in the existing politics of region their security lies in affiliating culturally and politically with larger identity such as Naga. Yet, they also feel the need to assert their cultural distinctiveness from the dominating Naga's concept of community. The case study of Khoibu is not only to show how a marginal community is disempowered, but more important is how such community negotiates with the dominant ethnic identities.

REFERENCES

Barth, Fredrik. (1969). Pathan identity and its maintenance. In *Ethnic Groups and Boundaries: The Social Organization of Cultural Difference*, ed. by Fredrik Barth: 117–34. Bergen-Oslo: Universities Forlaget, London: George Allen & Unwin.

Baruah, Sanjib. (2010). *Ethnonationalism in India: A Reader*. Delhi: Oxford University Press.

Beteille, Andre. (1998). The idea of indigenous people. *Current Anthropology* 39, 2. April: 187-91.

Calhoun, Craig (ed.). (1998). *Social Theory and the Politics of Identity*. London: Blackwell Publishing.

Colebrook, Claire. (2005). *Philosophy and Post-Structuralist Theory: From Kant to Deleuze*. Edinburgh: Edinburgh University Press.

Das, Rajat Kanti. (1985). *The Manipur Tribal Scene: Studies in Society and Change*. Delhi: Inter-India Publications.

_______. (1990). Emergence of ethnic process in Manipur: A reappraisal. In *Nationalism, Ethnicity and Cultural Identity in North-East India*, ed. by B. Pakem: Delhi: Omsons Publications.

Eaton, Richard M. (1997). Comparative history as world history: Religious conversion in modern India. *Journal of World History* 8, 2: 243-71.

Government of Manipur. (1981). *Folk Tales of Mayon-Monsang*. Imphal: Directorate for Development of Tribals and Backward Classes.

Kabui, Gangmumei. (1985). *Anal A Transborder Tribe of Manipur*. Delhi: Mittal Publications.

Khoibu Union. *Historical Background of Khoibu Tribe*. Unpublished: For private circulation.

Lehman, F.K. (1963). *The Structure of Chin Society: A Tribal People of Burma Adapted to a Non-Western Civilization*. Urbana: The University of Illinois Press.

Sharma, G. Amarjit. (2007). Cultural representation and politics of community: Rethinking identity formation in the North East region of India. Ph.D. Thesis, Jawaharlal Nehru University, Delhi.

2

Political Interpretation of Ritual

Case of *Lai Haraoba* of Manipur

Otojit Kshetrimayum

It is generally assumed that the importance of ritual action has declined in urbane conditions. On the contrary, the significance of ritual can be seen in every walk of life despite hectic urbanization process. For example, there has been a resurgence of *Lai Haraoba* in Manipur during the last few decades. There is a need to interrogate this perplexing and paradoxical aspect of ritualism. Here we try to analyse how the tradition of *Lai Haraoba*, a ritual for pleasing the gods, is being revived in Manipur and explore the socio-political factors responsible for it. Here we argue that the recent rise in the popularity of *Lai Haraoba* is associated with a cultural project that aims at developing it into a political force rather than just reviving the old Meitei customs. An attempt is also made to study the political significance of the ritual of *Lai Haraoba* in the Manipuri society and investigate how the political class tries to assert its power through the control of the management of the rituals.

The patterns of religious behaviour, like other patterns of social behaviour, are of great interest to sociologists, since they underscore the relationship between religion and society. Religious ritual is one of the dimensions of religious behaviour. The beliefs and ideals of different civilizations are often inscribed in their rituals more explicitly than in any other cultural trait, which gives the study of ritualism a greater sociological significance. What is more significant here is the dynamics surrounding the ritual not only in terms of its ritualistic or mythological connotation but also in terms of other variables such as revivalism, identity formation, regional politics, *etc*., which constitute important variables influencing its dynamics. The main argument that I would like to put forward in this study is that the rise in the number of religious rituals of *Lai Haraoba* is associated with the changing socio-political dynamics of the present Manipur. The increasing tendency for the establishment of the separate territory and administration of different tribes such as Nagas, Kukis, *etc.,* has a threat to the existing polity and territory of the State. This can be observed from two changing trends of religion and ritual. Firstly, the increase trend of *Lai Haraoba* in the State in general and urban area in particular indicates the growing awareness of the pre-Hindu identity of the Meiteis. Secondly, the ritualization of the tribal identity in the *Lai Haraoba* shows the basic urge of the Meitei to reassert the integral "Manipuri identity" of the pre-Hindu period. Apart from this, there also exists certain social and political dynamics associated with the *Umanglai* or *Lai Haraoba* at micro level.

Lai Haraoba: A Prologue

Lai Haraoba is a ritualistic festival, which the Meiteis have been observing since time immemorial. It is a ritual enactment of the creation of myth. It can also be referred to as a fertility cult. It mirrors the entire culture of Manipur and depicts the close affinities between the hill and plain people. It is, in fact, a combination of religious recitations, traditional music and dance, traditional social values and ancient cultural aspects (Panchani 1987, 132). It retains the original characteristics of the traditional Meitei religion (Brara 1998, 174). Celebrated in honour of the Sylvan deities known as *Umanglai*, the festival represents the worship of traditional deities and ancestors. It literally means, 'The pleasing of the god' (Shakespeare 1913, 81-9) or 'the merrymaking of the gods and goddesses' (Singh 1961, 30-4) or 'the god's rejoice' (Singh 1989, 11-8). One of the best examples of belief in the primal energies that the Meiteis have is evidenced from the enactment of *Lai Haraoba*. After the creation of the earth, *Asiba* (*Sanamahi*, the household deity), wondered how to create the living beings that would inhabit the earth. Seeing him at a loss, *Atiya Sidaba* (the Father Void) opened his mouth and showed him inside his mouth all the living beings that were to be created. *Aslba* was overjoyed and shouted "*hoi, hoi*", which came to be known as *Lai hoi laoba* (shouting of *hoi* by the *lai*, *i.e.*, the deity) and came to be known as '*Lai Haraoba*' (Brara 1998, 130). *Lai Haraoba* is celebrated in every *leikai* (locality), and every *khul*'s (village) *laipham* (abode of gods), but not everywhere at the same time (Brara 1998, 174). It is a community worship wherein the site of worship is situated outside the home, in the domain of the public.

Lai Haraoba is a religious event, which can only be understood in terms of the Meitei experience of the *lai*, the deities as the ultimate reality. The only secure basis for an adequate interpretation is one which takes seriously the spirituality of the *Lai Haraoba* as a ritual intended to bring about interaction between the world of the *Lais* and the human world, and to embrace both within the wholeness of a sacramental universe (Paratt and Paratt 1997, xiv-xv). Each festival is dedicated to a male and female deity as a couple who are addressed as *Lainingthou* and *Lairembi/Lairemma,* respectively. The theme of the festival is the celebration of life, its origin, fulfilment of the purpose of living and the continued existence through procreation. *Lai Haraoba* not only brings to the fore the sexual relationship between male and female but also celebrates it. The festival is celebrated every year, sometime in April or May in different parts of the State. The celebrations can spread from a few days to a month. It is a series of rituals. Each ritual is a combination of hymn, dance and music. The ritualistic performance is carried out through the medium of dance. This festival is perhaps the most indigenous of all the Meitei traditional festivals. It is also the one, which most closely preserves the ancient Manipuri culture and philosophy, and the importance of which is increasing with each passing day.

Dynamics of the Sacred and Profane

It is often seen in the context of Manipur that the dynamic elements in social change fail to be congruent with the cultural pattern. Rapid social change creates a tremendous hiatus between the cultural meaning of a ritual and the social scene. In keeping with this debate of change and continuity, the dynamics of sacred and profane can be discerned. Lately, with the exigency of time, the sacred space of *Lai*

Haraoba has started accommodating profane (secular) elements, mainly various genres of popular culture. Sacredness of *Lai Haraoba* can be of diverse forms, *viz.*, material, spiritual, spatial, *etc.*

The sacredness of the space can be divided into two. The first level is that of the sanctum sanctorum of the shrine, *laisang* (temple) which may vary from substantial brick building to a temporary thatched structure, which is renewed every year. The seats or bench for the *lais* are situated in the centre of the shrine with the offerings put in their correct positions around them. This space is a demarcated domain, which can be accessed only by the ritual functionaries. The devotees are allowed to enter till the threshold of the temple. The *laibung* (courtyard) is the area where the series of *Lai Haraoba* rituals take place and is in the second level of sacredness in terms of its accessibility. This is rectangular in shape whose three sides, leaving the side of the temple, are occupied by the leading members of the organising committee and the audience/devotees. The four corners represent the four guardian *lais*: *Thangjing* in the south-west, *Wangbren* in the south-east, *Marjing* in the north-east and *Koubru* in the north-west. The participants in their capacity as ritual performers other than the functionaries are part of the rituals taking place in this space.

With the rise of popular culture in the wider Manipuri society, this second level space has incorporated some secular elements. Such events take place only after all the rituals of the day have been completed. However, the sacredness of the space is still maintained, in the sense that, this is not intruded by the audience, though they are allowed to appreciate the performers in the forms of presenting money, *etc.*, with dignity and decorum. The secular items are mainly for the recreation of the audience and have nothing to do with the ritualistic content. The ritual functionaries have no role to play in these items. The organizers of *Lai Haraoba* have the authority of selection and rejection of such secular items, depending upon their tastes and ideological leanings. Such influx can be explained in the accommodative structure of *Lai Haraoba* itself. Being part of the whole social system, there is inevitability of its influence by the currents happening outside its domain. On the other hand, this is also the right vehicle to carry forward the popular culture as it has always been a medium to carry the tradition and philosophy of the Meiteis.

Such inclusion is also triggered by the practical problems, i.e., the declining of the interest of the people in pure ritualistic side of the *Lai Haraoba.* As a whole, claiming this process of inclusion of secular elements as secularization *per se* of *Lai Haraoba* is misleading. This is because the rituals and its contents have seen no sign of secularization down the ages. The relationship between the performances and the sacred space can be seen in terms of "contents" and "container", respectively. In the case of secular performances, the space remains as sacred as ever when the ritualistic performances are executed despite their secular contents.

Lately, there is a trend of decontextualization of the ritual dances of *Lai Haraoba* taking it out of the courtyard of a deity to other profane areas (including stages) for public performances. This is in congruence with the commercialization and commodification on one hand. On the other hand, it is also a response to the existential crisis of Manipuri society, which is trying to assert its identity and present it to the people who have no or less idea of its culture and tradition. This can be theoretically explained in conjunction with the dialectics of efficacy and entertainment. Efficacy of a performance refers to work for achieving a determined result; a link to an absent other; abolishing of time and creation of symbolic time; bringing of "other" here; possession of a performer in trance; participation by audience; believe of the audience on the performance itself; forbidding of criticism; and collective creativity. As opposed to this, entertainment yearns for fun; is meant only for those who are "here"; emphasises "now"; audience constitutes the "other"; performer knows what he is doing instead of being in trance; audience watches and appreciate the performance; criticism is encouraged and is an individual creativity. There is an increase in the degree of entertainment involved in these ritual dances when it is brought out of its actual context. But when in its ritual domain the degree of efficacy is more. Nevertheless, a performance whether of ritual or theatre or performing art is a braided structure of efficacy and entertainment and the genre is defined by the degree of their presence only.

Ritual, Politics and Power

The ritual of *Lai Haraoba* is the most important tradition of the

Meiteis. Its meaning can be analysed within a Durkheimian, functionalist framework, stressing the integrative force of such ritual, and the way in which it embodies and reflects, upholds and reinforces, deeply rooted, and widely held as popular values. In another tradition, the same ritual can be seen, not as expressing a publicly articulated expression of consensus, but as embodying the ruling elite consolidating its ideological or political dominance. David Kertzer demonstrates that ritual has always been and will continue to be an essential part of political life, used to symbolise, simplify and enhance political messages. He shows how ritual helps to build political organizations, how it is employed to create political legitimacy, how it fosters solidarity in the absence of political consensus, and how effective it can be in both defusing and inciting political conflict (Kertzer 1988). For ceremonial occasions as much as for great works of political theory,

> [...] to study the context...is not merely to gain additional information...; it is also to equip ourselves...with a way of gaining a greater insight into...its meaning than we can ever hope to achieve simply from reading the text itself (Skinner 1978, xii–xiv).

Thus, from this, we can arrive that in order to rediscover the meaning of *Lai Haraoba* during the contemporary period, it is necessary to relate it to the specific social, political, economic and cultural milieu within which it was actually performed.

According to David Cannadine, even if the text of a repeated ritual like a coronation remains unaltered over time, its "meaning" may change profoundly depending on the nature of the context. In an essentially static age, unchanging ritual might be a genuine reflection of, and reinforcement to, stability and consensus. But in a period of change, conflict or crisis, it might be deliberately unaltered so as to give an impression of continuity; community and comfort, despite overwhelming contextual evidence to the contrary (Cannadine 1994, 105). However, Eric Hobsbawm remarks that there are traditions, which appear or claim to be old but are often quite recent in origin and sometimes invented (Hobsbawm 1984, 1). With all these features in the setting we will now examine the link between the *Lai Haraoba* of Manipur, which is resurging in a great way in the present day and various social and political variables.

Ritual as Assertion of Identity

George Sorel brought to our notice how powerful myths can be for bringing about social transformation once they grip the imagination of the masses. When myths are collectively appropriated they are infinitely more powerful than when they are lodged in disaggregated individual consciousness (Gupta 1995, 9). Though revivalism in Manipur is very apparent today, this process had already been started even during the reign of King Garibniwaz (1709-48) when most of the Meitei culture and tradition had been destroyed and substituted by Hindu culture. Many people opposed the policy of the King. But the movement took a significant development in the 1930s. It was around 1930 that the Meiteis started discarding Vaishnavism and started reworshipping their ancient gods and practicing their traditional religion, which is called 'Meiteism' or 'Sanamahi religion' (Kabui 1990, 102). A young Meitei from Cachar named Naoria Phullo first started this movement. In order to investigate the ancient religion and culture of the Meitei, he founded a political group called *Apokpa Marup* (Association in the name of a Meitei ancestor deity) in Cachar in 1930. After Phullo's death, his followers in the Manipur valley initiated *Sanamahi* movement in 1945 and Pukhrambam Surchand became the President of this organization (Kangjia 1981, 18). Some of the important resolutions of this organization were as follows:

1. to revive the cultural heritage of the Meiteis;
2. to do research in the ancient history and other literatures of the Meiteis;
3. to revive the Meitei scripts;
4. to worship and chant religious hymns in the mother tongue (Manipuri/Meiteilon);
5. to strengthen the unity between the hill and plain people and to live together as brothers;
6. to strengthen the bond of unity among the Meiteis who are living inside and outside the territory of Manipur; and
7. to let the world know that a community known as Meitei has

> been in existence with their old distinct cultural and religious identity in the North-Eastern part of India (Kabui 1990, 102).

The objective of the movement is to revive the *Sanamahism*, the indigenous religion of Meiteis. They believe in *Atiya Mapu Sidaba, Pakhangba, Leimaren, Sanamahi* and other 363 host of the *Umanglai*. However, the sentiment of the movement is indicative more of a political trend than a regeneration of the religious belief. Several educated Meiteis have also denied calling the Sanamahi movement revivalist (Kabui 1974, 53-75). They believed that Manipur has been a culture of religious syncretism where the Brahmins and the Meiteis worship Meitei gods and Hindu gods. The two religious systems always co-exist. On the other hand, the Sanamahi followers assert that they have stopped all Hindu customs and follow purely Meitei system (Kabui 1990, 103).

This movement was geared to an extremist attempt towards the desanskritization of Meitei culture and the revival of Meitei heritage. The movement strongly opposed the Meitei identity with the Kshetriya caste and denied any link with the Indo-Aryan heritage claimed by the early promoters of Hinduism (Sirkar 1984, 121). It is primarily trying to revive and practice what is considered purely indigenous Meitei religion, culture, custom and the way of life. They want *maiba* and *maibi* to perform all their rituals and the other socio-religious functions in Meitei language. Brahmins have no role and no place for Bengali and Sanskrit languages in their socio-religious life. The movement leaders assert that they are neither anti-Hindu nor against any other religious community (Kabui 1990, 103). The movement aims at bringing in unity among the Meiteis and a closer relationship with the Nagas and the Kukis (the hill tribes of Manipur). The branches of this organization are scattered all over the valley while actively involving in reviving and popularising Meitei script, religion, language and other cultural activities. They claim that their members number more than 88,000 now (Kabui 1990, 104).

The most profound impact of the revivalism is on the cultural sphere of the Meiteis and the general awakening of their identity. The first trend of revivalism in Manipur can be seen in the restoration of Lainingthou Sanamahi at Haying Khongbal. Even the Government of Manipur recognised the necessity of reviving Meitei culture, religion and tradition. The Lainingthou Sanamahi Temple Board published a brochure on the occasion of "Mera Chaorel Houba", which fell on September 29, 1981. Irengbam Tompok, the then Deputy Chief Minister of Manipur sent a message referring to the need for revivalism. To quote his words:

> *I am glad to know that Lainingthou Sanamahi Temple Board is organizing to bring out a brochure on the day of Mera Chaorel Houba. I hope, this will bring the original and due faith and worship of the Meitei people. I wish every success of the Board* (LSTB 1981).

The Meiteis had neglected the worshipping of Panthoibi after Hinduism came in Manipur. In the last few years, the Meiteis have started establishing Panthoibi temples and worshipping her. In 1990, the number of Panthoibi worshippers and the temporary Panthoibi worshipping places (during the Durga Puja festival) has soared up. Revivalism of Meitei culture and religion can also be seen in the effort of the Meitei to worship the shrine of Mongba-Hanba in lieu of *Hanuman* image in the Mongba-Hanba Forest, which is also known as Mahabali Forest. The Meiteis claim that the term "Mahabali" and the "Temple of Hanuman" was brought into practice only during the time of King Garibniwaz. Before this the Meiteis called this place as "Mongba-Hanba Umang". Mongba-Hanba is one of the nine Laipungthous (mound god).

Another trend of Meitei revivalism was seen around the year 1980, when Meitei gods and goddesses substituted the Hindu gods and goddesses shrines at Nongmaiching hill. Before Hinduism came to Manipur, Meiteis had an early practice of climbing the Nongmaiching hill on the 28th *Lamda* (name of a Manipuri month, around February) to worship Nongpok Ningthou. This practice was originally known as *Chinggoi Iruppa*. It was during the time of King Garibniwaz that this festival was renamed *Baruni Snan* and all the worshipping places on this hill, which were known by Meitei names were converted into Hindu names. But in 1980, the Meitei National Front made a hard effort and succeeded in reviving the past tradition. That year names like "Mahadeva Shrine" came to be known as "Nongpok Ningthou Chingu Panganba Shrine". The pond known as

Saraswati Kunda became to be known by its original name "Shileima Ikon". The local newspaper *Janata* in its editorial column reviewed the situation.

> It is seen that in most of the temples, shrines and worshipping places of Manipur, Meiteism and Meitei form of worshipping have revived. The Meitei religion, which was about to disappear is showing its identity clearly (*Janata* 1980).

We will now try to locate the impact of revivalism on the observance of *Lai Haraoba*. In the *Lai Haraoba* festival certain programmes related with other religions have been dropped. Some years back, even scenes from *Ramayana* and *Mahabharata* were performed in front of the *Umanglais* during the *Lai Haraoba* festivals (Devi 1991, 89). Previously, there were a countable number of Umanglai shrines in different parts of Manipur. The number of local deities, which the Meiteis believe to protect them from supernatural evil forces, was also limited. Today, almost every locality seems to have either an *Umanglai* or a local deity. In the year 1991 almost everyday one can hear the sound of *Lai Haraoba* from one corner or the other of this State. Such interest shown by the Meiteis in their ancient gods and goddesses indicate their sense of cultural and religious revivalism (Devi 1991, 91-3).

The socio-political nexus that it enjoyed during the monarchial times seem to be a characteristic feature even today, *albeit* in a different context. Revivalist movement has brought to the fore an awareness of the "pre-Hindu" culture. The space afforded by the festival continues to assume political significance in the reinstating of a pre-Hindu identity. Its recent resurgence on a much grander and stylised scale assumes more than a cultural or religious revival. The resurgence may not have much to do with a growing religiousness towards the indigenous faith or belief systems. It, rather, reflects a consciousness of going back to and re-establishing cultural rootedness against the cultural homogenization associated with Pan-Indianism, which is seen as threatening to the interests of the smaller cultures.

Ritual as Solidarity

There are some historical evidences to support the close links between the Meiteis and the hill people. During coronation ceremonies the Meitei king and queen wore Naga dress and ornaments (Brara 1998, 3). The ritual *Lai Haraoba* also shows the relationship between the hill and the plain. God, the creator, comes down in Naga dress and meets his lover of the valley girl (Singh 1972, 26). There are also numerous instances where the Meitei kings married women from the hill tribes. An account of *Manipur Chronicle*, *Poireiton Khunthoklon,* records that the first king of Manipur Nongda Lairen Pakhangba married a tribal girl called Laisana (Constantine 1981, 21-2).

In the field of belief system also, the hills and the valley shares a legacy of commonality. The non-Christian tribals are animists; the forefathers of the Meiteis were also animistic in the ancient past. There are gods and goddesses that are commonly recognised both by the hill people and Meiteis. The hill tribes also worshipped Sanamahi, Leimarel and the Soraren (the Sky god), and every year, there is the Gang Nai festival among the Kabuis. The offerings to these gods consisted of meat, fish and wine, which are similar to the practices of the Meiteis in the past. The valley and hills also had the same food habits. But now the valley folks to some extent are no longer meat eaters (Singh 2000, 31-2). The process of Hinduization brought about a divide. Hinduised Meiteis categorised all the tribes as untouchables, who according to them lead lowly lives, take meat, drinks and offer the same to their gods, which the Meiteis practised earlier. Then, these two groups were further alienated when the hill people adopted Christianity in the early part of the nineteenth century (Brara 1998, 5).

Thus, a major example of social distance came in between these two groups of people. But there was apparently no racial difference between the valley dwellers and the hill people (Singh 1978, 62). Many of the British anthropologists also said that there are so many evidences that the Meiteis are the descendants of the Nagas. But successive invasions from the East and West had left a permanent mark on the population of the Meiteis. The above factors provided for a great cultural distance between the two groups. The cultural and linguistic differences, coupled with geographical isolation and political conditions determining the relationship between the groups were responsible for a distance wider than ever when the Meiteis became Hindus and the hill people became Christians (Singh 1978, 62-3).

To the orthodox Meitei Hindus, the tribals were considered like the untouchables of Hindu India and tribals were not allowed to enter inside the house of the Meitei Hindus. But the concept of purity and pollution was not found in reciprocal manner. The doors of the tribals were opened to the Meiteis. This social distance obtaining between the Meitei Hindus and Hill tribes of Manipur, which was ingrained for a few centuries, has remained unbridgeable to a certain extent today. There has also been rise of tribal political movement like the Naga movement for integration of all Naga-inhabited areas of the North-East India into a single political unit which includes the four hill district of Manipur and the Kuki movement demanding a Kuki homeland comprising the Kuki inhabited areas of Manipur.

Thus, there arises a need to remind and revive the close affinities of the people inhabiting the hill and plain people. One of the objectives of the Lainingthou Sanamahi movement or the Revivalist movement of the Meiteis is to strengthen the bond of unity between the hill and plain people of Manipur. The *Lai Haraoba* is a glaring instance of the close relationship between the hill and plain people. Someone in Tangkhul costume should represent Nongpok Ningthou and Panthoibi the divine couple without which the *Kanglei Haraoba* cannot be completed. On the last day of the Kanglei Haraoba a ritual known as *Tangkhul Thokpa* (appearance of Tangkhul) is to be performed. The Meiteis consider the ritual of *Lai Haraoba* as a mechanism for resolving internal contradiction between the hill and the plain people. No *Lai Haraoba* can end without the ritual of *Tangkhul Thokpa (saba)*. This is a dramatic ritual, which describes the meeting of the divine couple Nongpok Ningthou dressed in a Tangkhul costume and Panthoibi dressed as a Tangkhul girl. It can also be observed that Naga dances form a major part of the recreational items of *Lai Haraoba*.

Conclusion

Rituals associated with *Lai Haraoba*, though symbolic, aims at meeting some ends in the forms of the welfare of the people in the locality or village where the event is held, and also in terms of fertility (both reproduction and production). Beyond this, there is association of power politics where the authority (monarchy/state) tries to assert its power through the control of these rituals. This is what is termed as "efficacy" of the rituals as different from "entertainment" of other forms of performances. *Lai Haraoba* serves as a political symbol in the wake of regional political and cultural awareness. The political use of the ritual of *Lai Haraoba* at present is, in fact, a reassertion of the traditional ethos, which was confronted by alien cultures over the past 250 years.

The ritualization of Tangkhul (Naga) identity in the form of the *Tangkhul Thokpa* ritual in *Lai Haraoba* is a testimony of the close affinities between the hill and plain people. Therefore, the importance of *Lai Haraoba* gains momentum in this hour of crisis. It tries to harmonise the conflicting needs and aspirations of the Manipuri society. It attempts to generate a medium to reconnect the lost link. It also engenders certain sentiments that are advantageous to the Manipuri society. Consequently, we can see *Lai Haraoba* as essentially a collective attempt to resolve anxiety stemming from conflicts inherent in the Manipuri society.

Nonetheless, as we have mentioned above that there exists a code of inclusion-exclusion in the ceremony of *Lai Haraoba*. Therefore, it is doubtful of bringing all the communities of Manipur in general and the hill and plain people in particular in harmony as claimed by the adherents of Sanamahi movement. One cannot simply maintain that by mere performing the ritual of common origin myth and ritualization of other identity cannot entail a link without the actual participation of the "other". The resurgence of *Lai Haraoba* in the recent past can also be related to the emergence of ethnic political movements in Manipur. Thus we can identify this phenomenon as episodic and term it as "designer ritual" to borrow a term from Dipankar Gupta, which satisfies the ego of the observers.

REFERENCES

Brara, N.V. (1998). *Politics, Society and Cosmology in India's North East*. New Delhi: Oxford University Press.

Cannadine, David. (1994). *Aspects of Aristocracy: Grandeur and Decline in Modern Britain*. Yale: Yale University Press.

Constantine, R. (1981). *Manipur: Maids of Mountains*. Delhi: Lancers Publishers.

Devi, W. Ibemu. (1991). *Meitei Revivalism in Manipur*. M. Phil. Dissertation, Manipur University, Canchipur.

Gupta, Dipankar. (1995). *Political Sociology in India: Contemporary Trends*. New Delhi: Orient Longman.

Hobsbawm, Eric and Terrence Ranger (ed.). (1994). *The Invention of Tradition*. Cambridge: Cambridge University Press.

Janata. Imphal. 18th March, 1980.

Kabui, G. (1990). Socio-religious reform movement. In *History of Manipur (1826-1949)*, edited by Lal Dena: 89-117. Delhi: Orbit Publishers.

Kabui, G. (1974). Social and religious movement in Manipur in the 19th and 20th centuries. *Bulletin of the Division of History*. Imphal: Centre for the Post Graduate Studies, JNU.

Kangjia, G. (1981). Problems of Sanamahi religion after the World War II. *Kangleikhol*. March.

Kertzer, David I. (1988). *Ritual, Politics and Power*. London: Yale University Press.

Lainingthou Sanamahi Temple Board (LSTB). (1981). *Brochure*. Imphal. 25th September.

Panchani, C.S. (1987). *Manipur: Religion, Culture and Society*. New Delhi: Konark Publishers.

Paratt, S.N. and John Paratt. (1997). *The Pleasing of the Gods: Meitei Lai Haraoba*. New Delhi: Vikas Publishing House.

Shakespeare, J. (1913). The pleasing of the God Thangjing. *Man* 13, 50.

Singh, E. Nilakanta. (1961). Lai Haraoba. *Marg* 14, 4.

Singh, K.B. (1978). Social stratification and mobility in Manipur. In *North–East India: A Sociological Study*, ed. by S.M. Dubey. Delhi: Concept Publishing House.

Singh, L. Ibungohal and N. Khelchandra Singh. (1989). (Second edition). *Cheitharol Kumbaba*. Imphal: Manipur Sahitya Parishad.

Singh, Kh. Bijoykumar. (2000). *Hinduism among the Meiteis of Manipur: A Study of Continuity and Change*. M.Phil. Dissertation, Jawaharlal Nehru University, New Delhi.

Singh, Kh. Ratan Kumar. (2001). *Lai Haraoba of Manipur*. Imphal: Ph. Pratima

Singh, Kshetrimayum Imokanta. (2002). *The Impact of Craft of Theatre on the Aesthetic Culture of Society: A Study of Shumang Lila in Manipur*. M.Phil. Dissertation, Jawaharlal Nehru University, New Delhi.

Singh, N. Tombi. (1972). *Manipur: A Study*. Delhi: Rajesh Printing Press.

Sirkar, M. Chaki. (1984). *Feminism in a Traditional Society: Women of Manipur Valley*. New Delhi: Shakti Books.

Skinner, Q. (1978). *The Foundations of Modern Political Thought*. Cambridge: Cambridge University Press.

3

Lai Haraoba and Role of the *Maibis*[1]

Shilleima Chanu Naoroibam

The *Lai Haraoba* is the principal ritual festival celebrated to please and satisfy *Sanamahi* and mother Goddess *Lairembi* as well as *Umang Lais* as described in the latter part of the essay. *Lai Haraoba* is still survived as a principal ritual of pre-Vaisnavite faith and was not influenced by the Vaisnavism after the latter's emergence and domination in Manipur. The ritual ceremony of *Lai Haraoba* provided an arena for contest of power against patriarchal values, norms, beliefs, traditions, meanings, ideas and concepts. *Lai Haraoba* is not merely a ritual festival but it provides to resolve the gender contradictions in Manipur society by promoting idealised sex role models and stresses inter-sexual harmony by recognising two contrasting models for women—"ideal domestic women" and "unique and alternative lifestyle" as *maibi*. This essay examines the socio-religious roles of women and gender issues in *Lai Haraoba* (*lai* means God and *haraoba* means to rejoice) of *Sanamahi* religion (traditional religion) in Manipur.

Idealised domestic women in Manipur society are those women who fulfil the norms and values that are expected by patriarchal values, such as wearing of proper cloths like *fanek* (Sarong). It is worn by women of all social groups and ages throughout Manipur—covering body from chest to ankles by *mous* (married women). Generally the *mous* are not allowed to keep open their hair in public. They are not allowed to go out without any male members of the family at night and they are expected to do only domestic work. On the other hand,

Maibis need not fulfil the roles of the ideal women in private and public spheres as prescribed and expected by the patriarchal system. The *maibi* holds a special ritual status outside the norms of the patriarchal social framework for women. Yet they are an integral part of the Manipuri social system and are inclusive within the *salai* (clan) system. Though *maibi* form an integral part of the social system (Parratt 1980, 96), they provide a "unique and alternative life style".

In traditional Manipuri society, which accepted and practiced the *Sanamahi* religion, social and religious rituals, especially the *Lai Haraoba* are organised by *Maiba* (priest) and *Maibi* (priestess). In *Sanamahi* religion, *Umang Lais* (*Umang* means groves, which are regarded as "sacred or pure" and *lais* means gods) are given importance and are considered as the protector of life and property of the people. Hence, people organise *Lai Haraoba* for worshipping and celebrating *Umang Lais*. During the *Lai Haraoba,* which is the most important ritual component of the *Sanamahi* religion, various gods are invoked by the *maiba* and *maibi* to protect the people from the *saroi* (evil spirits). Similarly, people worshipped their *apokpa* (progenitors) in *Sanamahi* religion through an elaborate system of rituals and ceremonies called *apokpa khurumba* (prayers for progenitors). It is not a mere showing of honour and respect to their ancestors but is also a part of their belief in the immortality of soul, *Yaibirel Sidaba* (immortal supreme soul). People believe that after *siba* (death), their forefathers, look after the welfare of their children and that with proper ritual, they could be invoked to shower blessing upon them. So, *maiba* and *maibi* play an important and significant role in the various ritual ceremonies.

Origin and Socio-religious Role of *Maibis*

The meaning and origin of *maibi* is obscure. However, it is generally believed that they were in existence at least by the time of Pakhangba (33-154 AD)[2]. These ritual specialists held an exalted position and were an indispensable part of the society during the reign of Naothingkhong (653-763 AD). The coronation ceremony of the king was conducted with elaborate rituals under the strict supervision and guidance of these ritual specialists (Singh 1983, 49). The *Cheitharol kumbaba* records the institution of *maibism* as a part of evolution of the *Sanamahi* religion but worked as a branch of *pandit loishang* (the department of education) and account an earliest reference to *maibis* in curing the illness of Queen Meiteilcima Serambi, the wife of King Mungyamba (1562-1697) in 1570 AD (Singh and Singh 1969, 28). During the reign of Charairongba (1697-1709) the *maibis* were entrusted with the responsibility of superintendence of all religious activities and to reveal divine intentions (Singh 1976, 33 and108). While tracing the origin of the institution of *maibism*, Col. McCulloch also emphasised the existence of it from the very early period but he argued whether *maibis* have preserved their entire original characteristics since then cannot be certainly affirmed (McCulloch 1980, 21).

The terms *maiba* and *maibi* were used and translated by the early British officials who saw *Sanamahi* as a religion dominated by priest and priestess. Col. McCulloch (1844-1862) Political Agent of Manipur and T.C. Hodson (1901-1904) Assistant Political Agent of Manipur described *maiba* and *maibi* as merely the priest and the priestess (McCulloch 1980, 21; Hodson 1993, 109). Such an understanding was not entirely accurate. Apart from performing as priest and priestess, invoking and making offerings to *lais* (god and goddess), they also acted as physicians and midwives and also were expert singers and dancers who preserved the oral religious traditions and rituals. The *maibi* played a more prominent role in the rituals and she alone, when possessed by the *lai* (god), could deliver oracles. Traditionally the male *maiba* who experienced spirit possession had to dress in the women's clothing of the *maibi* (Shakespear 1993, 429). He would be called as a "male" *maibi* (here significantly, the term is *maibi* not *maiba*) and if he did convey an oracle, he would be addressed as *ima maibi* (mother *maibi*).

The ability of a *maibi* for accurate prediction heightened her status in the society. A *maibi* was always consulted by the kings before going to important expeditions and in times of crisis too, kings sought her advice, and then addressed her as *Ima* (mother). A *maibi* was responsible for performing propitiatory rites for the members of the royal family. Successful performance by a *maibi* often led to her speedy rise in status. She was generally gifted with cash and kind such as rice, other eatables, cloths, *etc.* A *maibi* made predictions by throwing *senkhai* (ancient coins) for her clients who included common people. She predicted the forthcoming well-being and dangers of an individual, of a clan and locality. She was considered to be able to predict exactly when, where and how the forthcoming things might happen. Historically speaking, she also performed propitiatory rites for them. Mornings were regarded as the best time for making predictions. Some *maibis* were known for their accurate predictions, other for their performing skills displayed during *Lai Haraoba* rituals and some others were renowned for their knowledge on traditional medicines (Kumar 2001, 67-9).

Maibi and Ritual Ceremony of *Lai Haraoba*

There are no rituals in *Lai Haraoba,* which can be performed without the ritual services of *maibi.* From the beginning to the end of the daily programme of the festival, the *maibis* remain busy performing various roles that range from oracle telling through the performance of rituals, to participation in various dances. The explanation of *Lai Haraoba* festival in this essay is based on my fieldwork during September-October 2009. Here, the festival is explained in detail from the first day to the end of the celebration so as to understand the *Lai Haraoba* and gender issue.

The first day of the *Lai Haraoba* celebration begins with *laifi shetpa* (clothing of the god). The *maibas* and the *maibis* start to prepare for *lai ikouba* (calling of the god from water) in which the principal *maibi* asks men and women to stand in two rows for the procession. Two *pakhangs* (bachelors) holding *thangs* (sword) are in the first row and second and third rows are comprised of four *leishabis* (maidens) who carry fans and wine goblets. Two *mous* carrying seat carpets and *sumbal* (rice pounding tools) are in the fourth row and in the fifth row are two men as *lai pubas* (bearer of gods). In the sixth row, there are two men holding two *chongs* (huge white umbrellas) over the god. At the first row an elderly woman stands holding an earthen water pitcher on her head and a group of *maibis* stands in a line in front of the procession.

During *Loichang jagoi* (awakening the god or welcome to the god) to *pena* music, the principal *maibi* gives two *ishaiphus* (earthen pots) to the two *lai pubas* (bearer of god). Then, *maibis* start dancing and leading the procession to a nearby pond where they fill the *ishaiphus* with water and dance *ishaiphu jagoi* i.e., rotating their arms with *ishaiphus* (earthen pots) in each hand and return the two earthen pots to the *lai pubas* (bearer of gods) taking out two lines of thread from them. Then, they, perform *laithemghat jagoi* (dance pleading the god to come out) while the *pena* (traditional musical instrument) keeps on playing. Suddenly, one of the *maibis* goes into a trance, *lai tongba,* (possessed by god) and delivers the *laipao* (the oracle or prophecy) and, then, later on she places the thread in the earthen pots and goes back to the temple. The old woman takes the water pitcher inside the altar room and two *maibis* take the thread out of the earthen pots and place them over the navels of the images. These ritual activities are called *hirifanba*. Married women dance to *pena* music while *maibis* carry several offerings for *saroikhangba* (to feed the evils) to different places of the village. Thus, the entire ritual *lai ikouba* (calling of god) completes on the first day. After the first day of the celebration, the *Lai Haraoba* follows the following daily schedule of rituals.

Daily schedule of rituals start with the *pena khongbas* (*pena* instrumentalists) singing specific songs awakening the god and the curtain of the altar is drawn open early in the morning. People from the surrounding localities come with their offerings and the *maibis* start singing and chanting and, then, go into *lai tongba* (possessed by god) delivering their *laipaos* (delivered an oracle) one after another. In the late afternoon, one can sense the festive mood of the people. Women and girls gathered wearing bright-colour *maiyeknaiba* (traditional colourful loin cloth), gold and gold-plated heavy jewellery and fine white transparent *inafi* (fine quality shawl) especially meant for the festival. Many *mous* wear the cotton *khwangchet* (wrapper) indicating the lineage of their husbands. Their foreheads are finely decorated with *chandana* (sandalwood paste) and they have flowers in their hair. Men wear white *pheijom* (traditional Manipuri *dhotis*) and *pungyat* (traditional Manipuri *kurtas*) with shawls over their shoulders. The *maibis* wear special ritual costumes over their everyday white dresses indicating their status in the *loishangs* (office). The evening rituals start usually around 3 p.m. and go by the following sequence.

Lailashingfa—everyday the *lais* (god) are dressed in new clothes by the *maibis* and they perform *leilangba* (collection of flowers) when several elderly men of distinguished status offer flowers to the god and distribute them first to the men and then to the women. After that *punglon jagoi* (dance in the rhythm of the drums) is performed by five *maibis* followed by a group of *machanupis* (little girls) facing the altar and no one is allowed to dance before the *maibis*. Later on, all the women join the dancing procession in groups for *thougal* (dedication dance). The *maibis* are followed by the group of *hanubis* (old women), *mous* (married women), *leishabis* (maidens) and *machanupis* (little girls) with gentle movements encircling the ritual ground while men come forward and offer gifts like cloths, money, *etc*. Immediately after the *thougal*, which lasts for about half an hour, a group of men, *maiba*, *pena khongbas* and *maibis* gather at the south-western part of the courtyard and perform *lai houba* (awakening of god).

After *lai houba*, the regular ritual is interrupted by a dance performance of *leima jagoi* (dance of mother goddess) presented by group of *leishabis* (maidens). The *Panthoibi jagoi* (dance of goddess *Panthoibi*) is dedicated to the divine mother *Panthoibi*, which is started by the *maibis* and later joined by the women for the *thougal*. Then, there is *anoirol* dance in which the *pena khongba* sings along with soft steps, raising their legs in swaying movements. The *maibis*, the *maibas* and women in different age groups follow the *pena khongba's* swaying movements by making a circle around the courtyard. The *Laipao* is the most important part of the daily ritual in which no one is allowed to leave the ritual ground after *laipao* (prophecy) has started. The *maibis* make arrangements for the *laipao* procession, which is very similar to the procession of *lai ikouba* (calling of god) ritual on the very first day of *lai haraoba*. As the procession starts, the *lai pubas* (bearer of god) go ahead of the *chong pubas*. The members of the *laipao* procession carry the same objects as they do for the *lai ikouba* (calling of god). During *laipao, maibis* perform a ritual called *loiching jagoi* (dance dedicated to creation), which means the joy of creation by holding *langthrei* (a small medicinal plant of Manipur) leaves between their fingers and making certain gestures of touching and stepping on the soft, newly created earth.

After *laipao,* there is *khoiyum jagoi* in which *maibis* dance with palms joined in the front with gentle swaying movements and walk forward in a circle. As the *maibis* lead the procession, women in different age groups join it. And then, *maibis* perform *khuttek mathek* (different movement of hands) dance to offer sixty four sequences of the *hakchang saba* (creation of the human body). Each of the movements is performed with specific hand gestures, the procession following with gentle steps. The 64 sequences of *hakchangshaba* are symbolised by different hand gestures. The *maibis* perform a dance asking for the soul of the body from *Guru Sidaba*, giving finishing touch to the making of the entire body.

Then, we have *mikon thakonba* (dance performed for the well-being of the community) in which *maiba* stand along with *maibis* and pray loudly for peace and harmony in the community. Later on, as a part of recreation, the *maibis* sing erotic songs symbolising sexual union of the *lai* and *lairembi* (god and goddess), which is called *pausha eshei.* Then the *maibis,* perform *pafal jagoi*, a dance which explains the sexual union of divine father and mother. While performing the dance, *maibis* have *lai tongba* and deliver oracle which is considered very important for the well-being of the community. So people, gather around the temple and listen it seriously. After the *maibis* came back to their senses, the *thang pubas* (sword bearers) bring two more *chongs* and join the two original *chong* bearers, and then, all of them gather in the middle of the arena which is known as *chongkhang naiba*. Two *maibis* take out the *hiri* (thread) that symbolises the souls of gods and perform *lairen mathek jagoi* (dance dedicated to god *Pakhangba*) a dance that reflects the *Pakhangba's* complex coiling and continuous movement. After about half an hour of the ritual, young boys and girls start *thabal chongba* (dancing with joining hands) encircling the huge ritual arena, keeping the ritual of *lairen mathek* going on in the centre. Then, *maibis* take the souls back to the images in the temple. A group of men and women stand on the porch and start *oakol louba* (prayer to God) in praise of the God, clapping in a joyous mood. While the song continues, young boys and girls go on dancing *thabalchongba* to band music, *dholak* and *pena*, which usually ends past midnight. In such a way, the ritual is continued for several days.

The last day of *Lai Haraoba* is the most important day. The last day also follows the same routine as in the previous days of the festival. On the last day of *Lai Haraoba, uugri hangel chongba* (dance symbolising the essence of sex) is performed in which a *maiba* stands at the centre of the ground and men and women hold a rope (previously dedicated to the god) forming a circle in alternate positions according to sex. Later on, *maibis* take out the ropes and men and women acting as couples move and *maiba* sings erotic songs teasing *lairembi*. After making two rounds of the circle, the two rows of people take to two different directions symbolising *kainaba* (divorce) and *punsinba* (union) of the deities. *Maibis* perform the rite of *lai loishinba* (ending ceremony) in which they declare that gods will go back to heaven and the white curtain is drawn in front of the altar and lights are extinguished. The day after *Lai Haraoba* athletic competitions like *mukna* (traditional wrestling), running race, *yubi* lakpi (rugby like game played with coconut), *thang ta* (play of sword and spear), polo, *etc*., are organised.

Understanding *Lai Haraoba* and Gender Roles

In fact, the series of rituals in *Lai Haraoba* promote patriarchal values, ethos and norms. However, rituals of *Lai Haraoba* do not seem to support male dominancy and female inferiority, which is a feature of patriarchal society. The *Lai Haraoba* proclaims the paramountcy of patriarchy. But its recognition of and emphasis on the female role is rather unexpected in a patriarchal society. The ritual recognises the dichotomy of the two sexes, who need to fulfil their prescribed obligations in their respective domains and, yet, need to depend on and co-operate with each other to ensure their obligations. The main focus of *Lai Haraoba* is on the perpetuation of the patriarchal norms and values in Manipur society. The rules of the *Piba's* (lineage head) eligibility; the model of the "ideal woman" as a participant in the core procession of the *Lai Haraoba*; married women wearing different colour *khwangchet* that represent their husband's lineage during the *Lai Haraoba*; the birth of the male baby and finally his naming by father, clearly support a patriarchal structure and protect its interest.

As far as women's participation is concerned, the most prominent of all the rituals is the *thougal* (dedication), in which large numbers of women participate, standing in order of their age. The *thougal* dance predominates in the ritual spectacle throughout the entire period. Traditionally, the *thougal* was always performed by women within a circle formed by men, an arrangement that is understandable in terms of male-female gender roles in the society. At present, the *thougal* is often performed exclusively by women independent of men.

The first ritual, *Lai Ikouba*, is very important for an understanding of the gender issues and roles among the people. In the *Lai Haraoba* procession celebrated for the well-being of a clan, the presence of the clan head and his wife as *lai* (god) bearer signify the principles of patriarchy. Both these bearers must conform to the clan rules of the ideal man and woman. The two men as *chong* bearers represent the male status. The young maidens and wives delineate their roles of providing nourishment and nurture. The *thang* men (sword bearers) signify male responsibility as warriors and protectors from external attack. Ahead of them all, walks an old woman holding a water pot symbolising the mother of all men and giver of the life sustaining force. The presence of the *maibi* leading the entire ritual and delivering her prophecy underlines a reverence for and reliance on female spiritual power to communicate with the other world. Male power is also evident at the beginning of the daily ritual of *lei langba* (floral tribute to god). But this is balanced immediately with a series of *thougal* dances representing women in various stages of men's admiration and adoration. From the very old to the very young, this is often expressed in warm and dignified exclamations and the offering of gifts such as clothes, money, *etc*., an expression of respect and appreciation. Dances depicting love legends reinforce the model of romantic love and the ideal relationship between husband and wife.

Celebration of the women's sexuality and fertility are a high point of the core ritual of *hakchangshaba*. In this ritual, the detailed description of the anatomy of the human body, labour pain, role of the midwife, reference to amniotic fluid as waves, appearance of the baby's head in the birth canal, the birth of the baby and cutting of umbilical cord are presented. The entire presentation has a dramatic and mystical aura that transcends the facts of mere biological truth, ultimately reaching a meta-social level. The fountain of milk, the life giving energy, is provided by the mother and the baby's name and his lineage identity are provided by the father. In *hakchangshaba* process, *maibis* perform the *khuttekmathek* dance to offer 64 sequences of the *hakchangshaba*. In the dance, each of the movements is performed with specific hand gestures with gentle steps. Women of different age groups follow the procession with a gentle dance step and rotating palm movements.

The *maibis* perform a series of theatrical dances enacting the phases in the progress of civilization. The performance of *chongkhongnaiba* dance signifies sexual union. The continuous coiling motion that symbolises king Pakhangba in *lairenmathek* dance is the timelessness of creation in its infinitude. The two lines of male and female deities separate to meet again and symbolises a battle of the two sexes in a playful encounter of divorce and union. The choreographic patterns suggest the form of the womb and the birth canal. While the continuous coiling motion proceeds smoothly in the middle of the courtyard, unmarried men and women hold hands to form a ring around it and perform the *thabal chongba* (dance with joining hands) dance. The whole spectacle represents the "moral community" transmitted from one generation to the next. In *Lai Haraoba*, the mutual co-operation and dependence of the genders are highlighted. The gender behaviour in *punshi ishei* (dance and song of the married couples), *ougri aongel* dance (dance and song symbolising the essence of sex), *hijing hirao* (enactment of boating race), *tangkhulshaba* (enactment of the legend of the divine erotic couple that signifies the blood relation between hill and valley) is full of friendliness, love and romance.

It is seen then that in *Lai Haraoba*, women are represented not only in terms of their reproductive potentials but also in their roles as daughter, wife and mother as expected in a patriarchal society. During the performance of the ritual ceremony, the four age grades in a woman's life cycle are depicted, which are associated with different socio-economic roles that women play in different phases of their lives. The productive role of unmarried girls in the agricultural economy is highlighted in the dramatic representation of *khutlang nupi taret*,[3] a team of seven daughters. The maidens while working in the field sing the *khutlang* songs. One can hardly claim this labour to be restricted only to the domestic domain. Such recognition of the daughters' collective labour in the community is indeed a rare patriarchal ritual. In *lamthokpa* (rituals relating to the celebration of God's coming out of the temple), an exuberant sword play by men is followed by women's gentle and graceful *thougal* dance. The gender role balance is ritualised here by emphasising the masculine role (warrior) in a social arena dominated by women. In fact, throughout *Lai Haraoba,* the wife's role is presented as that of a sexual partner as well as an economic contributor. And, in the latter productive role women outside the home are so elevated. Thus, *Lai Haraoba* presents prototypes of the male and female cultural models, encapsulating an ideal relationship between them. It highlights women's contribution to the perpetuation of society. And a remarkable feature of the festival is the recognition of women's role as economic partners as well as sexual partners and mothers as prescribed and expected by the patriarchal structure. On the other hand, it also provides an arena for the 'contest' and 'unique and alternative life style' as *maibis*.

Maibis as Unique and Alternative Status for Women

Lai Haraoba represents two opposing role models for women. On the one hand, there is the model of the "ideal, social and domestic woman"—woman as daughter, wife and mother as expected by the patriarchal structure. On the other, there is the "unique and alternative life style" as *maibis* who do not fulfil the expectation of the patriarchal system. *Maibis* are an indispensible part of the patriarchal society. But their presence signifies a "power relation" as Joan W. Scott describes, 'Gender is signifier of power relation' (Scott 1988, 10). The *Lai Haraoba,* which is celebrated in "public space" with dances and songs especially the erotic songs, is an attempt to explore the sexuality of the male and female. In fact, this ritual ceremony transcends, what Partha Chatterjee has described as two domains of "private" and "public" (Chatterjee 1993, 6). The *maibis* are not bound and confined to the "private" sphere. Their ritual activities during the celebration are reflection of women in the "public" sphere. The presence of *maibis* in a *Lai Haraoba* ritual is the most spectacular feature. From the beginning to the end, the principal *maibi* and her companions, as priestesses, not only conduct the ritual procedure but are also the most energetic performers who run the entire celebration in an intense and convincing manner. They attract the undivided attention of the spectators, and their ecstasy reaches a climax in trance, *laitongba* (possession by the spirit). A *maibi*'s oracular power has tremendous effect on the audience and sometimes exerts far-reaching influence upon the society. The power of prophecy uplifts a *maibi*'s status in the hierarchy, which involves rank and competition for professional success in society both of which belong generally to the man's world.

Sometimes, a woman would rebel against the family and the existing social order and find her way into a *maibi*'s life, a life, which promises her immense freedom in the extra-domestic domain, considerable social status and the prospect of good livelihood. These cases suggest a standard pattern of behaviour and none conforms to the normal sex and gender roles of Manipuri women.[4] Once a woman is ordained a *maibi*, she achieves a ritual status outside the expected norms of the patriarchal society. And her ritual immunity allows her a most liberated lifestyle unthinkable for an ordinary woman. She is her own mistress, having only the *lai*, the god as her guardian.

But a *maibi* is never called a "normal" or an "ideal" woman. People do not accept her role comfortably and it is accepted as the destiny of the exceptional women. Yet, a *maibi* is a chosen woman, a vehicle of supernatural power. She communicates on behalf of earthly people with the divine world. People are afraid to ignore her but still have an ambivalent attitude toward her. A ritual called *chuksaba* is performed when a *maibi* dies in order to prevent the birth of more *maibis* in the family. This is a reflection of the negative attitude of the people towards *maibis*. Thus, *maibis* suffer from social disgrace. Though they command respect as a ritual specialist addressed as *ima* (mother) by their clients in particular and public in general, their children do not suffer from any social stigma. Veneration for female spiritual power is formally recognised in the institution of *maibis*. Their professional world is directly attached to the central organization of *Sanamahi* religion.

Female spirit possession and female shamans are known to exist in several patriarchal societies. But patriarchal society do not consider them as part of the core religious system except in the simpler, less stratified society just above the hunting-gathering level. Spirit possession cults have been explained as an expression of rebellion or frustration of oppressed female in a male dominated patriarchal society. The most unusual feature in the institution of the *maibis* is that these women are ordained as priestess of the *Sanamahi* core religion. In a *Lai Haraoba*, the *maiba* and the principal *maibi* act as high priestess. The *maiba* follows a literate tradition based on his scriptural learning, a sphere exclusively reserved for the male and the *maibi* follows an oral tradition. But in *Sanamahism,* status and power might not have been invariably associated with scriptural studies. In the ritual field, the *maiba* and the *maibi* depend on each other's knowledge as colleagues. In the eyes of the society, the *maibi's* esoteric knowledge is by no means less valuable than the scriptural knowledge of the *maiba*. The respect and the recognition of the *maibi's* mystic power among the *maibas* and *maichou* (*pandit*) confirm this view. The *maibis* enjoy a central position in the *Sanamahi* ideological system. When challenged by Brahmanic culture, the *maibis* stood their ground and retained their prominent role.

Thus, what makes the institution of *maibis* different is that they are given elevated permanent status in recognition of their super power. They do not form a sub-culture; rather they are an integral part of the *Sanamahi* culture. *Maibis* are not considered social deviants, their role is accepted in the existing social order. A *maibi's* role can be seen as an alternative and unique lifestyle for women. It can be argued that this is an adjustment, which Manipur society makes to "gifted and uncontrolable" women in an institutionalised way. It does not hamper the social standard of Manipuri male-female behaviour, nor does it affect the ideal of a proper woman in the society. The *maibi's* liberated behaviour does not pose any threat to the male, who enjoys the advantages of the patriarchal system in the socio-political sphere. Women's spiritual superiority is, thus, accepted in an institutionalised manner and men do not have to lose their superiority standing in the social system.

The socio-religious status of the women in Manipur society is honourable due to her various and multifarious role as an "ideal and domesticated" women as prescribed and expected by patriarchy. *Maibi* is "unique and alternative life style" who does not fulfil the demands of patriarchy. The construction of two identities of woman, "ideal, social and domestic women" and *maibis*, symbolises a spirit to resolve the gender contestation in Manipuri society. The central role and position of the *maibis* in the *Lai Haraoba* festival of the *Sanamahi* religion reflects the negotiations of the women's power to that of patriarchal framework. *Maibis* always act in opposition to the standard behaviour laid down for domestic women. She doesn't engage herself in any domestic work except cooking her own meal. Generally, *maibis* are not expected to marry. If a woman marries after becoming *maibi* she cannot have a *luhongba* but only a *kainakatpa* (Thokachanba 1960, 101-08) and she lives at her husband's home like any other woman. Her husband treats her as an special person and has to offer wealth (bride price) to the *lai* (her guardian god). She sleeps at the right side of the bed, which in Manipuri society is normally used by her husband. She also has special days when she must abstain from sexual relations with her husband. The *maibis* do not take care of the children as normal mothers do, but only contribute economically towards their upkeep, as they receive gifts, like clothes, paddy, fruits, *etc.*, along with cash.

NOTES

1. The account of the Lai Haraoba festival is drawn from my fieldwork in which discussions with *maibi* Gulapmachu of Sanamahi Temple Board and Dhanu of the Royal Palace Imphal forms a major portion. Moreover, discussions with leading *Puya* expert Kangjia Mangang and scholars such as N. Shantikumar and N. Indramani deepened my understanding of the festival. Observation of the festival of Nongpok Ningthou Panthoibi Haraoba at Pungdongbam village and the Lainingthou Sanamahi Haraoba at Imphal in September-October 2009 greatly enriched my research on the festival of Lai Haraoba.
2. Interview with *Puya* expert Kangjia Mangang on October 7, 2009.
3. *Khutlang* is a traditional system of labour sharing, whose contemporary opposite is *Khutnek* or hired labour.
4. Interview with *maibi* Gulapmachu of Sanamahi Temple Board on October 4, 2009.

REFERENCES

Basanta, N. (1998). *Socio-economic Change in Manipur (1891–1947).* Imphal: Friends & Co.

Chatterjee, Partha. (1993). *The Nation and its Fragments—Colonial and Post Colonial Histories.* Delhi: Oxford University Press.

Ghosh, G.K. and Ghosh, Shukla. (1997). *Women of Manipur.* Delhi: A. P. H. Publication.

Hodson, T.C. (1993). *The Meitheis.* Delhi: Low Price Publications.

Kumar, Kh. Ratan. (2001). *Lai Haraoba of Manipur.* Imphal: M.I.K.

McCulloch, Col. (1980). *Account of the Valley of Munnipore and of the Hill Tribes.* Delhi: Gian Publications.

Parratt, S.N. (1980). *The Religion of Manipur: Beliefs, Rituals and Historical Developments.* Calcutta: Firma KLM Pvt. Ltd.

Mangang, S. Raghumani. (1988). *Meetei Law and Usage.* Imphal: Lanmei Thanbee Publications.

Scott, Joan W. (1988). *Gender and Politics of History.* Columbia University Press, New York.

Shakespear, J. (1913). The Religion of Manipur. *Transaction of the Folklore Society,* 24, 4.

Singh, Ch. Manihar. (ed. and tr.). (1983). *Naothingkhong Phambal Kaba* (coronation of Naothingkhong). Imphal: Manipur University Press.

Singh, L. Ibungohal and Singh, Ng. Khelchandra (ed.). (1969). *Cheitharol Kumbaba.* Imphal: Manipur Sahitya Parishad.

Singh, N. Ibobi. (1976). *The Manipur Administration (1709-1907).* Imphal: Friends & Co.

Sircar, Manjusri Chaki. (1984). *Feminism in a Traditional Society Women of Manipur.* Delhi: Shakti Book Depot.

Thokachanba, Th. (1960). *Thouram Pareng Asuba.* Imphal: Royal Press.

4
Thadou-Kuki World Views and Religious Practices before the Advent of Christianity

S. Nehkholun Haokip

The Thadou-Kuki traditional and religious practices are significant for it is considered to have characterised the Thadou-Kuki people's concept of origin, ethnicity, language and culture. The Thadou-Kuki traditions were not limited to beliefs in supernatural beings or ritualism of worship. It encompassed all the aspects of life, from farming to hunting, from travel to courtship. The Thadou-Kuki religious system seeks to explain the persistence of evil and suffering, and to portray the world as operating with some degree of ethical order and predictability. These ideas are expressed in sacred oral traditions, handed down from generation to generation through the performance of ritual acts of worship (dances and music) and through intensive periods of training in indigenous learning centres like the *SomBuh.* It is also a space where every youth of a village had to collectively spend time. The youths acquire knowledge about social customs and manners from the older groups of the *Soms*. The *SomBuh* serves as an institution of learning, discipline and other essential characters necessary for a man in future life and in the village administration. *SomBuh* serves as a space for organizing the youths to meet the exigencies of the society including rites and passage (Gangte 1993, 134). The Thadou-Kuki existential worlds of the pre-modern times were marked by both pragmatic values on one hand, and the other worldly conceptions on the other hand.

The supernatural and spiritual beliefs are important in the Thadou-Kuki religiosity. The concept of supernatural is embodied in *Chungmangpathen* by the Thadou-Kuki who is considered as the source of 'All Creations'. The creator is regarded as the highest benevolent entity signifying the perfect heavenly world. The idea of prosperity, growth and strength in life is, therefore, a gift of *Chungmangpathen* also known as *Chungmangpa*. The Thadou-Kuki social practices testify a rich heritage of communitylife quite substantially locating their worldviews often beyond hard core ambit of religiosity. They have established codes of food habits, farming, daily chores, hunting, clothing, family patterns, division of work, education, tradition of medical practices, etc. (Honignam 1963, 206) One of the interesting sites of The Thadou-Kuki society is its organisation of family as the basis of several other institutions. The Thadou-Kuki's family system confers the eldest son called *Upa* to live with his parents along with unmarried younger brothers and sisters compulsorily. Like many other social lineages, the Thadou-Kuki family is the smallest social unit in which every member of the family has an obligation to be fulfilled. Their religious beliefs and practices are not restricted only to one particular day of a week, be it Friday, Saturday or Sunday, but in all weekdays. The Thadou-Kuki religious values constitute the pre-Christianity world views (Gangte 1993, 161). The Thadou-Kuki believes that there is more than one god, however, they believe that one of the gods called *Chungmangpathen* is the Supreme god who created the world and all that is in the world. In the Thadou-Kuki religious systems, God (or the gods) after creation were not directly involved in human society or the individual lives of the people. In the Thadou-Kuki creation stories the gods were engaged in the creation of the world and all that is in the world, but after creation, the gods usually withdrew from direct contact with human beings.

One of the most important factors resulted in the development of polytheism among the Thadou-Kuki comes from the concept of 'power'. As the problem of survival is intimately bound up with economic resources, the egoistic tendency of man and his desire to acquire power or to be good hunter and fortunate in turn brings him to the belief that every object animates or inanimates, possesses a kinetic power for good or evil. The other probable speculation of the new breakthrough of polytheism in the society is the Egoistic

Emotion—fear or phobias (fear of poverty, fear of insanity, fear of illness etc.). Whatever elements of truth it contained in the above gestures, it is difficult to give a synthetic conclusion of the same as the problem is very complex one. In fairness, it is the long religious-cultural or mystic-magical experiences of the people under varying social environments that gave birth to this pluralistic world view (Haokip 2006, 14).

The idea of disinterested god does not make the supernatural unimportant in the *Thadou-Kuki* mythology. The super natural God (who ascended to heaven or sky after creation) and spiritual realm constitute an important aspect of their religiosity. It is believed that 'spirits' come as an interlocutor between the creator and humans. The spirits are directly engaged in the lives of human beings, and can act as intermediaries between God and humans (Lienhatdt 1966, 144). Spirits in the *Thadou-Kuki* religious traditions share some of the same characteristics of angels in the Christian, Islamic and Jewish traditions. Good spirits help to protect against illness and misfortune and assist humans by providing rain needed for crops, fish and game animals used for food. However, not all spirits are good, some spirits are viewed as evil and are believed to be responsible for illness, premature death, and other forms of suffering and death, and other forms of suffering and misfortunes.

Animism, a belief in spirits or the spiritual world, or the world of spirits, is central to the *Thadou-Kuki* religion. Spirits (like Angels and demons in the Jewish, Islamic, and Christian traditions) directly communicate with and impact the lives of human beings, as individuals and as communities. Good spirits provide protection against harm, misfortune, and disease, heal illness, and provide children, rain for crops, fish, and wild game, and protection for livestock. The realizations of these blessings are dependent on the appropriate behaviour on the part of individuals. Good behaviour, according to *Thadou-Kuki* religious beliefs, includes following and practicing values and behaviour established by society and culture, participation in religious rituals and practices, and proper respect for family, neighbours, and community. Good spirits can be divided into the following categories:

Human spirits: They believe that people continue to live, through their spirits, after death. These spirits are often referred to as ancestral spirits. It is believed that spirits of the ancestors remain very interested in the welfare and growth of their families and communities. The Thadou-Kuki religion segments ancestral spirits into two groups. First, *The recently dead ancestors*: After the death of an elder his or her spirits remains actively interested and engaged in the life of their family and community for many years. They intercede with God on the behalf of their communities. However, if individual members of their families or communities as a group engage in inappropriate behaviour, the ancestors show their displeasure by withdrawing their protection—their willingness to seek God's blessings on their descendants. The ancestors hope that illness and misfortune will be seen as a warning and result in people and communities stopping the inappropriate and offensive behaviours. The *Thadou-Kuki* religions hold that following social and cultural norms and values is the only way to guarantee security and prosperity.[1] Second, *The spirit of the long dead*: as time passes, the spirits of the recently dead gradually withdraw from the lives of their descendants and communities.

It is believed that these spirits live with God. However, some ancestral spirits remain actively engaged for many generations. This is particularly true of the spirits of important individuals. It is believed that the spirits of great rulers or founders of nations maintain their interest and power for a long time, perhaps centuries after their deaths. These ancestors are most interested in promoting the longevity of their kingdoms, nations and communities. As with the regular ancestral spirits, these spirits intervene to protect their communities. In the *Thadou-Kuki* religion, ancestors are not gods and they are not worshipped, but just as living elders are given great respect, so the spirits of the ancestors are remembered and respected. Moreover, ancestral spirits are not feared. Although their blessings are important to personal and community well-being, appropriate behaviour is all that is required to maintain social harmony, longevity and ancestral contentment.

In other words, the *Thadou-Kuki* religious tradition holds that just as there is good in the world, there is also an evil one called *malignant spirits*. Malignant spirits intervene when there are instances of:

- Inappropriate behaviour on the part of individuals or communities,

- The malignant spirits comprise of:
  - (i) *Joumi* (Dangerous male spirit), it is said to be elastic, which can become very tall and can also be short at will. The *Joumi* is very fond of chicken, it kills by throttling their neck and suck its blood dried.
  - (ii) *Gamhoise* (The king of evil, who inhabits in the densest forest on the highest mountain top), (Shakespear 1912, 200) if a sickness is believed to be caused by *'Gamhoise'* immediately a buffalo is to be offered along with rice-beer, a cock and unboiled rice to appease him.
  - (iii) *Gamkau* (Jungle ghost): *Gamkau* is an evil spirit of a particular place of a jungle which can cause serious illness to the person who meets such spirit (Gangte 1993, 162).
  - (iv) *Maltong*: A widow, lame, lone and cruel. Anyone who worships and pleases her was blessed with immediate and rapid richness but soon loss the richness even up to the extent of having no heir to the worshipper.
  - (v) *Kulsamnu*: Female spirit or witch who is in charge to keep up the souls of the individuals who passes her residential quarters on their way to *Mithikho* (dead men's village). It was traditionally believed that any soul proceed to *Mithikho* after death shall pass the residential quarters of *Kulsamnu*. She cannot stop the soul to *Mithikho* but can delay the journey if she is not appeased. Moreover, it is believed that she dare not keep up the souls of person who had performed *Chon, Sa Ai, Chang Ai* and lovers.
  - (vi) *Kaose*: The Thadou-Kuki live in a great dread of vampires, men who can so project their astral bodies as to enter into those they wish to and devour their internal organs, particularly the liver and heart, and can also convert such person into a different personality, changing the voice, the behaviour and strength. The Meiteis of Manipur also have a similar belief in the vampires which they called 'Hingchabi', and the Maori also believe in vampires who send its *atua* to enter a man's body and slowly eat away his vitals (Shaw 1928, 155).

(vii) *Lhadam* (Men's Souls/Ghosts resulting from unnatural death): Lhadam is the soul of death people which remains on the earth before going to dead man's abode. It is the common belief that the soul of death people does not go to *mithikho* directly. It stays on this world for certain days and maintained the family chain and continues to visit their house at night and produced some sounds but invisible (Haokip 2006, 14).

(viii) *Lhangnel* (A python having seven nostrils who lives under water): the python can control human beings and animals through its vibrating magical power. It was believed that this python had seven nostrils and lives under water.

(ix) *Lashi* (Female fairies), who appeared in the form of a beautiful ladies and are regarded to be the care-takers of wild life. It is believed that young man who falls in love with these alluring fairies often became famous hunters in their life time.

(x) *Chomnu*: Female spirit, who is believed to be physically short. She seldom causes any trouble to mankind and considered to be harmless spirit.

(xi) *Kaomei*: Evil spirit that flies at night like a fire—fly in a much bigger volume of fire-ball. It is a dangerous spirit for if anyone be it human being or animal resulted in severe illness.

The evil spirits are believed to be responsible for causing much of the misfortune that individuals and communities suffer. The Thadou-Kuki society has specially trained professionals who through special medicines and communication skills intercede with the ancestral spirits to provide protection against the evil spirits. Here comes in the institution of priests. One of the most important functions of priests is to officiate religious ceremonies and rituals. Religious ceremonies and rituals are important in maintaining religious and cultural traditions. Ritual ceremonies celebrating birth, transition to adulthood, marriage, death, planting and harvesting, hunting, or commemorating the life of a deceased ancestor, are vital to maintaining a close-knit community. Such rituals also help to reinforce values and appropriate behaviour within the community. The priests who officiates at these rituals and ceremonies, plays a central role in fostering a strong and united community. A priest will enter into a trance during which time it is believed that the spirit of the ancestor enters or possesses the body of the priest. During the period of possession, the ancestor directly communicates with the priest, using him as a medium of information to the people.

The rites of propitiation can be classified into, rites of appeasement and rites of warding off evil spirits which cause illness. The rite of appeasement involves the offering of animal or the image of *So'longnupa* (slaves), *Sel* (*mithuna*), *Dakpi* (gong), *Sumeng* (coin), *Khechang* (beads), etc., (Shaw 1928, 77) which are made of clay as these articles are regarded as valuable in terms of wealth and treasure. The rite of expelling or warding off evil spirits is in the display of magical power on which the sorcerer chants magical words having the force of energy (Singkhakhai 1976, 182).The sacrificial rites and the rites of propitiation of the *Thadou-Kuki* can be classified into three, *viz.*, personal rites; household rites and communal rites. The sacrifices can be further detailed into the following aspects—

Chang Kithoi Na (Individual sacrifices)

(a) *KhaolangKithoi*: If a person is suffering from symptoms of Typhoid or Pneumonia, the traditional *Thadou-Kuki* term sickness, *i.e.*, *Khaolhang* is used, which means that individual's health is endangered. Either a *Mithuna* is sacrificed but if for some reason it can be substituted by the skull of another *Mithuna*. Therefore, the rite of *Khaolang* is sometimes called '*SielLuhomKithoi*', rites of *Mithuna* skull, (Mangneh 2011) .

(b) *InneolangKithoi*: The word *Inneolang* denotes the direction from where the particular sickness comes and *Kithoi* is the rite of propitiation. Therefore, the rite is performed to appease the spirit that dwelt in the direction of *Inneo*, who is supposed to cause the illness.

(c) *LhanlamKha*: If the spirit of a deceased person frequently appears in the dreams of anyone of his family members, a ceremony called *LhanlamKha* is performed. The simple meaning of *LhanlamKha* is blocking the path of the graveyard. It is a precautionary measure taken to prevent or protect the dreamer from death.

(d) *KilhaLah Na*: This ritual is performed for a person who is suffering from the symptom of yellow fever or Yawndise. It is common belief that the soul of such person have been seized and detained by the demon called *Gamhoise.*

(e) *Milha Kou*: The literal meaning of *Milha Kou* is the calling of the human soul. The practice of calling of human soul is of two types:

(i) *Milha Kou* (The calling of sick a person's soul): If a person falls sick after returning from hunting or from the *jhum* field, it is believed that the person has lost his soul. Therefore, a ritual expert (*Thempu*) is immediately summoned to call back the wandered soul; otherwise the sick person may die (Shakespear 1912, 76)

(ii) *Chalha Kou* (Calling the souls of offspring): If a woman is not blessed with offspring her father performed a sacrifice called *Chalha Kou* or *LhaLho* which means, interceding for blessings of his daughter, so that she may be blessed with sons and daughters.

(f) *GulDoi*: If a person suffered from sores and sore throat, it is believed that this sickness was caused due to a snake having been seen or killed. Thus, this rite is performed by killing a dog or a fowl, which is offering it in sacrifice.

(g) *Golkhen Na/Ui-ThengKithoi/Ui-Hap Vat*: If a person has a sudden change of behaviour and becomes abnormal in his way of talking and movement. It is believed that the person is under the influence of an evil spirit called '*ThilhaVop*'. The *Thempu* has to perform a sacrifice and ward off the evil spirit that has possessed the sick man.

(h) *Hampalangleh Pasanlang*: If a child is found suffering from the symptoms of whooping-cough, measles, high fever, etc. it is believed that the sickness is caused by an evil spirit. In this ritualistic sacrifice, grasses of different varieties were sometimes collected and used as items of sacrifice. The ritual-abstention such as, social restraint, personal purification, etc., is continued for five days.

Household Rituals

(a) ***Indoi Sacrifices***: The word *Indoi* literally means 'house-magic' and is the name given to the deity of individual household. It is, therefore, a family deity, though community is invited to take part in various phases of its activities, when a particular man performs *Indoi* worship. Each householder has its own *Indoi.* It serves the whole family so long as the members all live under the one roof, but on separation new *Indoi* may be made. There is no fixed time for this and it is usually done when a separate household feels that it is suffering from a lack of health or of wealth and that the want of the *Indoi* may be the cause. Thus, in making a new *Indoi* the *Thempu* plays an important part[2].

With the agricultural year beginning a fresh commitment to *Chungmangpathen* represented by the *Indoi* was proclaimed, accompanied at the same time by prayers for blessings for the ensuing days of the year. The three occasions when *Indoi* is invoked are: the first time induction of *Indoi* for a new household; second—the annual re-enactment day known as Hun; third—the occasional therapeutic rituals when *Indoi* is taken down from the original place called *Sutkhom* which is the main pillar of a house in the middle row which has to be a *se tree* for the occasion. In the events of sickness in the family, preparation is made for a ritual involving a sacrifice of a pig or *mithuna.* On this occasion the *Indoi* is taken down from its original place, hung on the *Doikhom* (sacred post) until all the necessary and obligatory rituals are performed. The prayer offered on this occasion is the same as those on the other two occasions, except that on this occasion there is a prayer also for the recovery of the ailing person. When an illness besets one or more of a family the Indoi is meticulously inspected so as to determine what sacrifice is required (Chongloi 2008, 204).

(b) ***Hun Ceremony***: Having placed an *Indoi* in each household the annual re-enactment ceremony known as *Hun* is observed. No precise date was fixed for this, but usually it fell at the time between the month of May and the beginning of June. The Thadou-Kuki being *jhum* cultivators determined the dates of their ceremonies and rituals in relation to their agricultural calendar. *Hun* was fixed at the time when paddy sown on the *jhum* field sprouted, which in *Thadou-Kuki* terminology is called *Changnel Kai Phat*. The occasion was very important in religious terms but was also a time of merriment and festivities. Wine and other delectable items are especially prepared for the occasion. The healthiest piglet was kept aside and reared, slaughtered on this occasion and a blameless white cock too completed the requirement. Having instituted an *Indoi* each household regularly observed the annual re-enactment ceremony known as *Hun*.

The *Thadou-Kuki* being a *jhum* cultivator determined much of their ceremonies and rituals in relation to their agricultural activities. *Hun* was fixed at the time when paddy sown on the *jhum* field sprouted out from the ground, which in *Thadou-Kuki* terminology is called *Changnel Kai Phat*.

(c) ***Daiphu Ritual***: After a field has been harvested, *Daiphu* is performed. For this the *Thempu* has to make small earthen images of the following:

- *Saipi Ha Som* (Ten Elephant's teeth),
- *So'longNupa* (Slaves),
- *Vengke* (Patridge),
- *Thoche* (Squirrel),
- *Sel Lim Som* (Ten Mithuna),
- *KhichangSom* (Ten pieces of ear beads), and
- *Dahcha Lim Som* (Ten gongs).

(d) ***Chang NungahPoh*** (Paddy Deity): This is a kind of paddy that is grown sparingly in the field. These paddy plants never sprout flowers or fruits. People believed that this variety of paddy helped increase the fertility of the soil, and also augmented production. When such paddy plants grow in the midst of other paddy plants, they are carefully preserved, even after the harvesting as they believed that it is a sign of prosperity and good fortune. This particular paddy plant grows very rarely. If by chance such a plant grows, it is reverently treated and certain rituals are observed in order to appease the 'Deity' in charge of paddy, such paddy is called *Chang Nungah* and it is worshipped.

(e) *The Ancestor Sacrifice*: The sacrifice performed to the Ancestor-god is a part of the household rites, and it is of two kinds. One is the annual sacrifice of offering a pig, the other is the sacrifice of a *Mithuna*. The main objective behind performing such sacrifices is to seek the generous beneficence of the ancestor Gog and to appease the spirits of the dead or else they may call down malignant spirit of illness on the family members who have not propitiated them. The rite of ancestor sacrifices involves animals, cereal offering and *jupi* (rice beer) offering. The preparation for these offerings needs some ritual services. The rite demands the participation of household councils that consists of *Tuchas* and *Bechas*. The sacrificial rite of *Pu-Sa* (appeasement of ancestor spirit) ritual is to be performed at night in the innermost of the house belief to be a sacred place (the sacred place covers the space between the main post called *Sutpi* and the back post; where common people are not allowed to enter. The animal to be sacrificed is taken out from its den. After being cleansed, it is brought in and placed by the main post called *sutpi*. The priest after saying his ritual prayer, kill the animal (usually a pig) by piercing through the left armpit, aiming at the heart with a sharpen instrument called *satul* (bamboo spike). The carcass is then cut into pieces in accordance with the customs and boiled. The organ part of the lung, heart, kidney, intestine, etc., are boiled in the innermost of the house, which is specially meant for the household councils, the priest and chief of the village. While the remaining meats are boiled in the family hearth, this is for the people who come to participate in the ritual (Singkhakhai 1976, 174)

(f) ***Chon:*** This festival or ritual considered auspicious and everything concerning it has to be done seven times. Seven *mithuna* are to be killed and everything else must be in multiples of seven. Even the songs, dances and genealogical trees had to be repeated seven times. Even after the death of such persons who performed *chon* the corpses had to be carried around in, *Shang-Lai* (a litter constructed with bamboos bound together to make a kind of make-shift platform on which the deceased could be laid) seven times and everything pertaining to burial rites had to be done seven times. Thus, the performance of the *chon* gave the soul of that person a premier seat in ***mithikho*** and ensured eternal happiness.

(g) ***Tolso Rituals:*** Those who have done and accomplished the series of the feasts of merits become *tolso*. To achieve this status was not easy as feast of merit were a great incidence on income as they involved a fairly large number of religious rites to be performed prior to the ceremony, each of which entailed heavy expenditure. The various feasts of merits that a person performed before he became a *tolso* were, *Sa Ai, Gal Ai, Chang Ai, Chon. Tolso*—the term literally means to pass through lengthy and elaborate rituals to undergo a vigorous test of self-abstinence, social restraint, personal purification etc. Thus, a man has to attain the ritual status of purification by stages of ritual performances as it refers to a person's preparedness to perform *Sa Ai* or *Chang Ai*. The prospective candidate conveys his/her intention to concerned persons (priest, chief, *upa*, etc.) through his ***becha*** (a person whom an ego considers good and who can go along with him and can stand by him in times of joy and sorrow, may be chosen as 'Becha'. A man of wisdom, versed in customary laws and tradition, and expert in interpreting culture and social values, may be selected. This last relative is to act and speak on behalf of an ego, as if he is the ego himself, and is, therefore, regarded as the representative of the ego when discharging the social, economic, religious or political obligations). Then the *becha* made a formal announcement called '*Tolso Ding Kigo*'. Thereafter, the man and his wife had to undergo a vigorous test of self-abstinence, social restraint, personal purification, etc. The ritual was carried out in three different stages.

This ritual lasts for one day during which time the candidate undergoes various disciplinary norms and dietary abstinence. The spouse also joins in the ordeal but on less stricter scale. In the second stage, the *becha* of the family informs the *Thempu* of their intention to proceed with the self-purification rites to attain purity physically, mentally and spiritually.

The Communal or Village Rites

(a) ***Aikam Ritual:*** *Aikam* is a kind of village ceremony performed by the village *Thempu*, when any rumour or news comes about of any fatal epidemic like cholera, typhoid, etc., that has taken its toll in neighbouring villages. The idea behind performing this ceremony is in fact, to block or resist the spread of this fatal epidemic in the village. The *Aikam* ritual is both mandatory as well as propitiatory.[2]

(b) ***Khopi Changlha Kou***: The ceremony of *Khopi Changlha Kou* is normally held in the month of May, when the sowing of paddy seeds in the *jhum* fields is over. The animal to be sacrificed in this ritual must be a full grown pig, and the ceremonial rites are to be held at the residence of the *Haosapu* (chief). The day of *Changlha Kou* is observed by the entire village as taboo, called *KhopiZechang*. No one is allowed to enter or leave the village. Everyone of the village must be gathered at the residence of the Chief, drinking and singing takes place throughout the day.

(c) ***Salha Kou*:** The ceremony of *Salha Kou* ritual is performed once in a year. The animal to be sacrificed must be a blameless cock of any colour, to be donated by the chief of the village. The ceremonial rites are officiated by the village priest. Eventually, the main sacrificial service of *Salha Kou* ritual is performed in the evening after sunset. The priest, with a cock in his hand sits under the sacred post called *Doikhom*, which is erected in front of the Chief's house. Then, he throttles the cock which is to be sacrificed, and calls upon the soul-spirit of all the known animals. The Thempu likewise saying "All you beasts of the world and flying game taste this *ju*, it is much better than any *ju* you all will ever have, so come here for it when you are thirsty." By this it is meant that they will be enticed to come to that village and the hunter will kill them all (Shaw 1928, 81).

(d) ***KhopiDoiLha***: This is sending-off or setting free of the unseen evil-spirits, who are supposed to be in the village. It is a kind of village purification service performed once in a year by every *Thadou-Kuki* village. It is believed that illness of all kinds are caused by the evil-spirits called *Thilhas*. Ceremonies are to be performed to appease them and to request them to leave the village. The ceremony is to be officiated by the village Priest called *KhoThempu* on behalf of the entire village.

(e) ***KhopiChangkut***: On the arrival of this auspicious day the village Priest along with the village elders goes to the outskirt of the village called *Khomoul* and performs a village purification service called *KhopiThensoNa*. On the very spot where the ritual of purification is to be held, the priest then throttles a cock. After the arrival of the *Thempu* at the residence of the *HaosaPu*, who first commences the sucking of the ready-made rice-beer that is in the jar, through a pipe called *Don* (it is made out of bamboo). The priest declared that, whosoever observed ritual-abstention thereafter was free to eat, drink and freely mix with other people of the village.

(f) ***Khongchoi Ceremony***: This concerns the religious rites involving young boys and girls directly in competition with the evil spirit, called *Thilha*, in order to earn fame for the *Lom* or young organization of the village, which combines with a sense of festivity. On the day of the ceremony the *Lom* members, start congregating at the *Khomol*. Khomol is small hillock near the entrance of the village from the main road. It is very important in the village life of the Thadou-Kukis in view of the political, social, economic, religious, significance being attached to it. It is also a place for performing all sorts of rites, like *Kithoi* (appeasement of the evil spirit), and a place for welcoming the guests or a point up to which guest or persons leaving the village on tours area seen off.

Conclusion

The *Thadou-Kuki* social practices reflect not only the religiosity and myths, but it also embodies practical values of socio, economic and cultural organisation as a collective and community. Nevertheless, the *Thadou-Kuki* world views remained highly entangled in the other worldly interpretation of its traditions and pre-modern experience. One can sense the similar trajectory being invoked in the conception of 'Chungmang Pathen' as the God creator. Interestingly, there is an agency communication that connects the worldly and the other worldly affairs which in turn shapes the humans. The worship of 'Indoi' as God of household symbolizes the importance of diverse activities with regard to the social, cultural, economic and political aspects of their lives. Ancestor worship is also a common feature in the Thadou-Kuki tradition and religion. Their belief and respect for the ancestral spirits constitute the source of their prosperity and security of the families and community. For instance, the *Thadou-Kuki* customary practices continue to somewhere hover around the traditional values, may it be birth, marriage, or death. Highlighting the importance and appropriation of such values, T.S. Gangte states that, "as man knows nothing of his future, he either invents or adopts certain manner of ritual or *rite de passages* to palliate his unseen fears which are tinged with idea that constitute part of his life-style in grassing into their culture and religion that may determine his outlook as well". The Thaduo-Kuki rich cultural heritage of their religious philosophy insight has been attempted to preserve. Nevertheless, it can be argued that the modern rendering of Thadou-Kuki tradition and myths, before or even after Christianity, fails to properly demarcate between what constitutes tradition and religiosity on one hand, and scientific social formation today, on the other.

NOTES

1. This information is taken out from the interview with Mangneh Haokip, former Thempu of Theusse village, interviewed on the 12th July 2011.
2. Letsat Haokip, Changpikot Village, whose father was "Thempu", interviewed on the 25th September, 2011.

REFERENCES

Chongloi, Hemkhochon. (2008). *Indoi: A Study of Primal Kuki Religious Symbolism in the Hermeneutical Framework of MirceaEliade*: Published by Rev. Dr. Ashish Amos, Indian Society for Promoting Christian Knowledge. P.O. 1585, Kashmiri Gate, Delhi.

Gangte, T.S. (1993). *The Kukis of Manipur:* Gyan Publishing House, New Delhi.

Honigman, John. (1963). *Understanding of Culture*: Published by Harper & Row, New Delhi.

Haokip, D. Sonkhojang. (2006). *A Study on the Traditional Religion of the Kuki before the Advent of Christianity* (Unpublished Ph.D. Thesis, Manipur University), Manipur.

Lienhatdt, Godfrey. (1966). *Social Anthropology*. New Delhi: Oxford University Press.

Shakespear, J. (1912). *The Lushei Kuki Clans*: Published by Mrs. Suman Lata, Cultural Publishing House, Delhi.

Shaw, William. (1928). *Notes on the Thadou Kukis*: Cultural Publishing House. Delhi.

Singkhakhai. (1976). *Zo People and their Culture*. (Published by Khampu Hatzaw, Printed at BCPW, 85-PDA Complex, Lamphelpat, Imphal, 1976).

Part – II
A Take On Manipur's Economy

5

Economic Question in Manipur and the Discourse of Development

Malem Ningthouja

Spectre of economic crisis looms over Manipur. It is a crisis characterised by:

> (a) dependence on import of commodity and money; (b) capital accumulation at the market dominantly controlled by Indian monopolists that drain wealth of the people; (c) corruption, misappropriation and mismanagement of fund by State machinery and (d) comparative underdevelopment that has serious repercussion upon peasants and workers. The crisis has emanated as a result of Manipur's unfavourable balance of exchange with the outside world. In other words, British colonial intervention had destroyed the traditional foundation of Manipur's economy by bringing Manipur within the ambit of capitalist economy. Moreover, there was no qualitative change to Manipur's economy after the State was merged to the Dominion of India in 1949. As a result, the material conditions necessary for sustainable development are completely underdeveloped. Except for some cosmetic fabrications in and around Imphal and a class who have vested interests in continuing misplaced developmental projects, majority of the people are impoverished and nature of the economy is dependent and aid driven without any productive bases essential for development. This becomes

self evident in the revenue generation capacity of the State. The State has generated meagre revenue in each passing year, which is far below the development propaganda of the State and Central Government. Economic crisis in Manipur contradicts the development discourse that is being projected in teleological fabrication widely articulated by the ruling class since the 1990s. For the purpose of analysis, one may concentrate on the year 1972. The year 1972 is important primarily for the reason that the Indian State had identified statehood with political autonomy, *i.e.*, relative economic development (Nehru 1972).

According to government reports, Manipur is being economically integrated under Indian Five Year Plans. The growth in the number of towns from 1 in 1951 to 33 in 2001 is being construed as one of the several indicators of economic growth. Similarly, comparative analysis of Indian's Five Year Plans have suggested a steady rise in the gross estimates of expenditure or plan outlay, particularly after the fourth Five Year Plans. According to the Planning Commission of India, plan outlay for Manipur has increased from ₹ 2 crore, to ₹ 6 crore, to ₹ 12.9 crore, ₹ 30.25 crore, in the first four Five Year Plans, respectively.

An increase in fund inflow from the Centre becomes apparent by 1980, e.g., Central assistance to Manipur was increased from ₹ 286.51 crore in the Sixth Plan, to ₹ 613.44 crore in the Seventh Plan, to ₹ 1,230.03 crore in the Eighth Plan, to ₹ 2,493.61 (agreed) in the Ninth Plan and to ₹ 2,166.42 (projected) in the Tenth Plan. Plan outlay for Manipur was increased dramatically from ₹ 30.25 crore in the Fourth Five Year Plans to ₹ 430.00 crore in the Seventh Five Year Plans (1985-1990). It was further increased to ₹ 1787.01 crore (Expenditure) in the Ninth Five Year Plans and further to ₹ 2804.00 crore (Outlay) in the Tenth Five Year Plans. Manipur enjoys status of Special Areas, i.e., strategically important and backward. It has been financially improving through funding and finance management under various institutions such as the North Eastern Development Finance Corporation Limited (NEDFI), established on August 9, 1995 and the Ministry of Development of North Eastern Region (DONER), established in September 2001 and accorded the status of a full-fledged ministry on May 2004.

Apart from receiving investment under Border Area Development Programme; funds and grants for Manipur are allocated through Non-Lapsable Central Pool of Resources. By the time an Indo-ASEAN Car Rally for promotion of international trade was held in November 2004 Manipur was an economic focus for successful implementation of India's Look East Policy. The government reports, therefore, argue for an endless effort to improve economic condition of Manipur and has projected positive growth in the North Eastern Region Vision 2020 (Government of India 2008).

Economy sans Welfare

Contrary to the apparent growth as mentioned in the fabricated teleology, reading against the grain of parallel reports and researches illustrates a comparatively backward economy for Manipur. Economic condition of Manipur since 1949 has been one of dependency to New Delhi's grants-in-aid. During this period various mega industrial establishments costing thousands of crore of rupees to the Consolidated Fund of India were set up in the privileged States of mainland India (United Committee Manipur 2002, 7). However, till the Fifth Five-Year Plan Manipur got ₹ 1.55, 6.25, 12.88, 30.15 crore, respectively, *i.e.*, too little for development (Laishram 1998, 8). And the corrupt Indian bureaucrats did not fully utilise it for any initial stage of development (Mohendro 2005). According to a report of the Institute for Human Development, New Delhi, Manipur as late as 2005 continued to be largely underdeveloped and agrarian with a weak industrial sector and inflated services sector. Analysing growth and inter-state disparities in India would reveal that Manipur which had a low ranking economy in the period beginning with 1960-61 had continued to be in lower rank throughout the period till 1995-96 (Dasgupta and others 2000, 2413-422).

As far as developmental and fiscal deficit are concerned, 'the share of the State in the All India Net Domestic Product remained stagnant at 0.2 per cent almost throughout the period 1991-92 to 2001-02 (Manipur State Development Report 2006). Till 1993 Manipur has deficit of ₹ 158 crore (Laishram 1998, 8). As a result

Manipur's own resources in the Tenth Five Year Plans had been ₹ – (minus) 362.42 crore. As far as Per Capita Income of Manipur is concerned, in 1980-81 (at 1993-94 Prices) it stood at ₹ 4901 against all India income of ₹ 5,966; and correspondingly at ₹ 5,811 against ₹ 8,759 in 1993-94; ₹ 8,963 against ₹ 12,496 in 2001-02 respectively. According to the 55th Round of the National Sample Survey Organization's (NSSO) (July 1999 to June 2000), though the poverty ratio had declined, the number of poor had increased from 5.86 lakhs in 1973-1974 to 7.19 lakhs in 1999-2000 (Government of Manipur 2006b, 198). The NSSO 61st Round survey report showed a drastic decline in the number of poverty to 3.95 lakhs in 2004-2005.

The decline is based on new methodology of poverty estimation and does not calculate actual number of poor persons whose access to basic requirements of subsistence has been fast declining. Unemployment problem among the youths in Manipur increases beyond controllable stage (Khomba 1996, 32-3). Financial position of Manipur is considerably weakened and it had resulted in the State treasuries remaining open for a few days only in each month. The Manipur Rifles had attempted a *coup* in 1999 against the government for delaying their monthly salary for months. In 2002 the State was no longer in a position to discharge its debt-service burden (Forum of Chief Minister 2000). In the year 2005 out of the total number of 356,193 households living in Manipur 115,600 households were living at the Below Poverty Line (Government of Manipur 2006a).

The overall economic condition remains precarious and unfavourable to growth. The situation contradicts concept of economic welfare. Firstly, economic welfare is a material condition founded on productive utilization of natural resource and human skills. Productive production is required in order to create and supply effective demands. Secondly, production constitutes the backbone of political economy and as such, good governance is a precondition for effective production. The two understandings suggest that polity and economy are interplaying. In a seemingly democratic Indian sub-continent, the Government of India that is in absolute control over Manipur political economy, therefore, has the obligation to invest for the economic welfare of the people of Manipur. This expectation is not being fulfilled by the Indian rulers whose primary interest in Manipur is concentration and centralization of capital.

Resources Exploited

There has been gradual loss of control over the natural resources (including land) as resources are regularly deregulated by the Indian laws and transferred for private use to outsiders, government agencies and corporate bodies for economic exploitation without the consent of the people. Natural resources are no longer absolutely managed by the local people. "Forests are stripped off, water bodies destroyed by pollution, hydro-electricity generation projects and neglect of maintenance" (Centre for Organization and Research, Manipur 1999).

Controversial capitalist projects are being forcibly imposed. Capitalist "projects" become controversial as a result of State violation of existing democratic norms such as Environment Impact Assessment, Environment Management Plan, Official Clearance, Public Hearing, absence of favourable compensation and rehabilitation scheme, etc., lack of transparency and public accountability (Citizens' Concern for Dams and Development 2005), corruption, mismanagement, brutal suppression of public opinion as reported in the *Sangai Express* on July 10, 2008 and arbitrary imposition of projects under the protection of police or paramilitary forces (Yumnam 2008). The controversial Loktak Hydro Electric Power Project and Tipaimukh Dam are few of the several examples to illustrate.

Firstly, the Loktak Hydro Electric Project, better known as Loktak Project, has been a matter of controversy for several years for various reasons. There is visible lack of a Scientific Integrated Approach to systematic utilization of multiple advantages thrown open by Loktak Lake (State of Environment Report Manipur 2009). A total of 27,404.94 acres of agricultural land are lost as a result of the Loktak Project. The Government of India has not planned compensation to landowners whose cultivating fields are being destroyed.

Secondly, the controversial Tipaimukh is being protested on the ground that it is a typical Special Economic Zone for capitalist profiteering and would lead to displacement and destructions. According to a protest raised in 2001:

> The proposed 162.80 metres high dam... will result in permanent submergence of 275.50 sq kms of land surface in

> Manipur…The Manipur people's constitutional rights were circumvented by secret approval of the project given during the period of central rule in Manipur (in 2001)… The government of Manipur is at present attempting to sign the Memorandum of Understanding (MoU) with North Eastern Electric Power Corporation Limited without the participation of the people, particularly the affected people of Tamenglong district (Pamei 2001, 1054 and 1148).

The Government of Manipur, however, has decided to go ahead with the project at any cost without taking into consideration public opinion. In March 2009 it had demanded provision of four battalions of central paramilitary forces in addition to the pre-existing forces for deployment in the Tipaimukh project areas (reported in *Hueiyen News Service* on March 4, 2009). What becomes apparent is that "developmental aggression" instituted by the Indian rulers contradicts "sustainable development". Whereas "developmental aggression" represents capitalist material interest, "sustainable development" required for survival and progress of the people of Manipur remains suppressed.

Uprooted Agriculture

In so far as the agriculture sector is concerned, attention given to agricultural development in Manipur from the first to Fourth Five Year Plan was inadequate for a possible breakthrough into an advanced agriculture. The Plan outlay in agriculture from first to fourth Five Year Plans were ₹ 6.30; 109.51; 190.97 and 305.66 lakhs, respectively. According to Mohendro "one cannot possibly expect 'impressive' turn with this meagre outlay" (Mohendro 2005). There was absence of a sound development strategy for agriculture planning guided by the principles of; increased productivity of land and labour; bringing more land under cultivation; and increased intensity of cropping. No attempt was made to strengthen agricultural base in terms of improvement in: Land system, Irrigation, Technology and Institutional finance, etc. No census of land holdings and cultivation was carried out for Manipur as late as 1955.

According to a survey published in 2006 only eight per cent of the total geographical area of Manipur was under agricultural operations, compared to the all India average of 64 per cent. The spread of irrigation was comparatively poor with merely 15.5 per cent of the total area cultivated being under irrigation. The share of agriculture in the State's income had declined from 45.6 per cent in 1980-81 to 24.7 per cent in 2003-04. Compared to the all India trend, this is a far more steep fall since the share of the primary sector in the State fell from 49 per cent in 1980-81 to 29.2 per cent in 2003-04 as against 38 per cent to 25 per cent at the all-India level (Institute for Human Development 2006).

Disinvested Industrial Sector

In so far as the issue of industry is concerned, there could have been industrial expansion, at least in the handloom and silk sectors. An analysis of the trend of resource committed to the so-called industrial development conveys a message of less attention. The token outlay of ₹ 0.60 lakh in the First Five Year Plan was increased to ₹ 13.06 lakh and ₹ 49.39 lakh only in the Second and Third Five Year Plans respectively. During the Third Five Year Plans sericulture received a share of ₹ 4.29 lakh only as plan allocation. No skill inventory was prepared.

The Industrial Policy of 1982 had laid primary emphasis on development of large and medium industries. The Industries Policy of 1990 focused mainly on the development of the small-scale sector. However, the State has not witnessed desired level of industrial activity (Government of Manipur 1996a). A new State Industrial Policy was announced in 1996 (Government of Manipur 1996b). But it was silent on the necessity for earmarked industrial area. It has not declared any Industrial Area. Industrialization attempts existed on paper only. No substantial investment in constant capital for manufacturing industrial take off had been initiated by the government.

Between 1993-94 and 2000-01 the share of industry in Net State Domestic Product had risen from 15.73 per cent to 21.75 per cent, *i.e.*, 38.27 per cent increase. The increase is due to high share of the construction sub-sector in Manipur, e.g., dams, office buildings and beautification projects. However, Manipur has the largest decline in the share of manufacturing in Net State Domestic Product from 4.61

per cent in 1980-81 to 3.37 per cent in 1995-96. In 1996-97, the state accounted for the lowest share in the North-East region (Institute for Human Development 2006, 147).

High Level Commission Report to the Prime Minister, Government of India in 1997 has stressed that North-East (Manipur inclusive) has little or no plan resources but heavily indebted in spite of high per capita Plan outlays and subventions. Huge establishment costs exceed State revenue collections as government service provides the sole and certainly the principal avenue of employment. In terms of per capita State domestic product or other standard development indices such as power, road length or hospital beds, the North-East ranks well below the national average (Planning Commission 1997). In 2002, out of 2,014 registered factories, 80.3 per cent were rice mills, another 10.3 per cent were saw-mills and 4.76 per cent were oil mills. The situation had not improved as late as 2005. In 2005 most of the State-owned corporations have been closed. 30.86 per cent of Small Scale Industry units were sick and 90 per cent of micro enterprises were in trouble (State of Environment Report Manipur 2009).

Marginal Peasants and Workers

Internal dynamics within Manipur between the period 1950 and 2000 has revealed dramatic rise in population, for instance, according to 2001 Census, Manipur population had increased from 577,635 in 1951 to 2,388,634 and corresponding rise in the consumption demand. Slow growth in the productive scale, slow scale improvement in the instrument of production and disproportionate investment could not satisfy demands.

In other words, the Indian State has expected private investment when a backward State such as Manipur requires for tremendous investment in the public sector. As a result, productive capacity of Manipur has not been built up over a long period of time and, therefore, its resource base could not be effectively moulded into the development process of Manipur (United Committee Manipur 2002, 29-30). Foodgrains, pulses, vegetables, fruits, edible oil, milk and dairy products, medicines, snacks, liquor, poultry products, fish and almost all varieties of consumer goods of day-to-day usage are imported from outside. Effective demand for import leads to export of money that has been largely derived from service sector and New Delhi's grants-in-aid, loan and fund. As a result of comparative decline in local production, heavy reliance on import drains the wealth of the people.

A steady rise in the number of poors has been indicated by the growth of marginal workers. According to the official record the number of marginal workers has increased from 40,469 in 1981; to 66,621 in 1991 and to 285,849 in 2001. During 1991-2001, the growth rate of marginal workers was 329 per cent. As far as the incidence of unemployment is concerned, in 1983 the rate of unemployment was 0.4 per cent of the total labour force. It was increased to 1.8 per cent in 1993-94; further increased to 3.5 per cent in 1999-2000. According to the department of Planning, Government of Manipur, 21.58 per cent of the total population remained unemployed in 2005 (4.93 lakhs) (State of Environment Report Manipur 2009).

The growth in the number of poors is more or less explained by relative decline in landholding and continuous breaking down of household based subsistence economy. According to the report of the Statistics Department, Government of Manipur (Government of Manipur 2002), the actual area under landholding increased by 16,734 hectares between the years 1975 and 1990. The increase was due to deforestation and claiming of hitherto unclaimed lands. However, total number of holders increases by 281 only. Analysing the break-up of the statistics reveals that actual area of large holding (above 10 hectares) increased by 45 hectares only and the number of holders by 9 only. The corresponding figure was 4,685 hectares and 811 holders in case of medium (between 4 and 9.99 hectares); and 6,082 hectares and 1,392 holders in case of semi-medium (between 2 and 3.99 hectares) respectively. The statistics reveals a different picture in case of both the small (between 1 and 1.99) and marginal (below 1 hectare) holdings. In case of small holdings the actual area under this category increased by 6109 hectares but the number of holders declined by 343 holders.

In case of marginal holding, both the area under this category and number of holders declined by 187 hectares and 1,588 holders respectively. The overall area of holding of marginal class in 1990-91 was 37,820 hectares against the overall area under holding, *i.e.*

174,981. It is likely that a sizable number of the marginal holders completely parted with land but some new holders emerged all of a sudden taking over those parted lands or pre-existing richer holders bought up the parted land. There appeared to be transfer of holdings without causing much affect in the number of holders in that category. A further fall in the number of the holders of the marginal category was rather prevented due to three reasons.

Firstly, in compliance with the customary distribution of property for inheritance among family members, those big holders above the level of marginal produced both small and marginal holders through fragmentation. Secondly, fragmentation by those in the category of marginal produced the category of marginal only. Thirdly, family without any inheritance of holding became better off and started buying up land of that category. An equally alarming situation has been the process of fragmentation of land for the purpose of housing or conversion of household gardens into construction. It creates disequilibrium in the household subsistence economy that relies heavily on it for garden products such as vegetables, firewood, fruits, flowers, pulses, grains, roots, stems and other daily requirements.

In the central valley areas the total area declined between 1985 and 2001 under the category of forest, non-agricultural usage area, barren, pasture or grazing, miscellaneous cultivable waste land, fallows was 20,760 hectares. Since the area actually used for sowing crops during the corresponding period increased by 15,305 hectares only it is likely that the rest of the 5,454 hectares were used for the purpose of constructing roads, government and private complexes, institutions and settlement areas. There is considerable scale of conversion of household gardens for construction purposes. People could not afford to build multi-storeyed buildings and, therefore, they extended their construction horizontally on ground floor. One then has to increasingly depend on market for everything including those items hitherto available in respective household gardens. And since the opportunity to earn money is always scarce, material interest of the large chunk of poor remains unfulfilled.

Accumulation of Capital

Bribery, corruption and misappropriation of fund at the superstructure level and service sectors have deprived a large chunk of peasants and workers of positive investment, free and fair resource mobilization, and other economic opportunities. Capital is dominantly accumulated by a microscopic section of the population basically composed of political leaders, bureaucrats, contractors, smugglers, absentee landlords and professional groups who ran profiteering enterprises and indulge in corruption and misappropriation of fund. The microscopic section is least affected by the economic crisis as long as they are agents and promoter of finance imperialism. The capital they accumulate is not invested for economic growth rather they spend it to meet expenses for imports, extravagant activities and for leading lavish lifestyles.

Capital accumulation also takes place in the market by outsider monopolists. Most of the consumer goods available in Manipur markets are imported through a network of commercial entrepreneurs of outsider who were in control of the Manipur economy. Profit that went into their treasury is repatriated to their respective home States beyond Manipur. Therefore, in the absence of local production, cosmetic financial incentives or funds that is allocated for Manipur remains under circulation in the market for few days and is siphoned off beyond Manipur through the unfavourable balance of exchange and monopolists. The economy, therefore, is unfavourable to progressive growth. Gradual decline in the economy has corresponding impact on peasants and workers. Economic experience of Manipur since 1949 has been the steady rise in the number of poors and marginalization of large segment of population.

Conclusion

There is an organic relation between politics and economy. The material relation between India and Manipur may be understood in terms of the theoretical understanding of Alexander Buzuev (1990) who had argued for "Economic inequality of nations". Manipur plays a subjective role under the capitalist economy of India. The forced merger of Manipur in the Dominion of India in 1949 was a threshold in placing both India and Manipur into an economic arrangement instituted and governed by the Indian ruling class. It was a threshold to conditioning interrelated phenomenon: firstly, Indian ruling class creating a military base in Manipur for accumulation of super profit from North-East region and South-East Asian Countries; secondly, Manipur's loss of political autonomy and a corresponding loss of control over economy and a *vice versa*; and thirdly growing impoverishment of a large chunk of the population. The Indian State's aggressive attitude towards imposing finance imperialism explains its failure to respond positively to public yearning for accountability, transparency, compensation, rehabilitation, equitable distribution of profits and a role in the decision making. It becomes crucial factor in shaping the prevailing economic condition in Manipur.

REFERENCES

Buzuev, Alexander. 1990. *Economic Inequality of Nations.* Moscow: Progress Publishers.

Centre for Organization and Research Education, Manipur. 1999. *Criticism and Constructive Submission Regarding the Study on Treaties, Agreements and Other Constructive Arrangements between States and Indigenous Populations.* Report submitted to the Sub-Commission on the Prevention of Discrimination and Protection of Minorities, Commission on Human Rights, UN.

Citizens' Concern for Dams and Development. 2005. *A Critical Analysis of the Capital Project, Manipur*. Imphal: CCDD.

Dasgupta, Dipankar, Pradip Maiti, Robin Mukherjee, Subrata Sarkar, Subhendu Chakrabarti. 2000. Growth and inter-State disparities in India. *Economic and Political Weekly,* 35, 27. July: 1-7.

Forum of Chief Minister of the North Eastern States. 2000. *Memorandum* submitted to the Prime Minister on June 21.

Government of India. *Third Five Year Plan.* New Delhi: Planning Commission of India.

_______. *Tenth Five Year Plans.* New Delhi: Planning Commission of India.

Government of Manipur. 2002. *Statistical Handbook of Manipur 2002.* Imphal: Directorate of Economics and Statistics.

_______. 2006b. *Economic Survey Manipur* 2005-2006. Imphal: Directorate of Economic & Statistics.

Government of Manipur, 1996a. *Industrial Policy of Manipur.* Imphal: Directorate of Economic & Statistics.

_______. 1996b. *Manipur Gazette.* December 9. Imphal: Secretariat.

_______. 2006a. *Annual Administrative Report of Manipur: 2005-2006.* Imphal: Secretariat.

Institute for Human Development. 2006. *Manipur State Development Report.* New Delhi: Institute for Human Development.

Khomba, P. Khuman. 1996. Youth's mental unrest in Manipur in *Youths' Mental Unrest in Manipur,* Imphal: National Research Centre.

Laishram, Dhanabir. 1998. *Chaokhatpa Khunnai Amasung Meeyam* (Developed Society and the People). Imphal: Centre for Progress of Manipuri People.

Mohendro, N. Development Experience in Manipur: 1891-1969 and the lost Article of Self-reliance. <http://www.manipuronline.com/Economy/November2005/self-reliance03_2.htm.>

Nehru, B.K. 1972. Inaugural Address to the Manipur Legislative Assembly on March 30, 1972. http://manipurassembly.nic.in/html/gov_add72.htm (accessed on 7 April 2014)

Pamei, Aram, 2001. Havoc of Tipaimukh High Dam Project. *Economic and Political Weekly* 36, 13. March 31–April 6.

Planning Commission of India. 1997. Transforming the Northeast: Tackling backlogs in basic minimum services and infrastructural needs. High Level Commission Report submitted to the Prime Minister, Government of India on 7th March.

State of Environment Report Manipur.<http://www.manenvis.nic.in/stateprofile1.pdf.>

United Committee Manipur (UCM). 2002. *A draft policy to protect and uphold the unique historical features, existing historical boundary and also for bringing emotional integration of the people of Manipur to achieve faster economic development of the State.* Imphal: UCM.

Yumnam, Jiten 2008. '*Mapithel Dam amidst Militaristic Development in Manipur'* in the Imphal Free Press, 6 December, Imphal.

6
Perspective on the Industrial Scenario in Manipur

K. Gyanendra Singh

Plan Allocation and Strategy of Industrialization

After independence on August 15, 1947 and subsequent merger to the Indian Union, the erstwhile princely state of Manipur came under the purview of the centralised planned development under the Five Year Plans. Since inception, planned development emphasised the importance of three sectors, *viz.*, transport and communications, social and community services and agriculture. Besides, a significant share of the Plan resources was also allocated for development of water, power and irrigation. The Plan expenditure in industrial sector was, however, very low to the tune of less than three per cent of the total plan expenditure up to the Third Plan. During the Fourth and Fifth Plan expenditure had increased to about 7 per cent. Since the Sixth Plan expenditure has declined to less than six per cent of the total expenditure. The outlays for the industrial sector in Tenth and Eleventh Plans are 11.87 per cent and 8.05 per cent of the total outlay, respectively (Singh 2011). Thus, the strategy of planned development in Manipur focused on the growth of infrastructure and social and community services rather than on the real sectors of the economy. Although this strategy of development is understandable in the initial years of independence, the strategy has not changed much even after 63 years of independence.

With such a meagre expenditure and outlay, it is hard to make any dent for the improvement of the industrial sector in the State. Moreover, given the geographical location, topography and the resource base of the State, the cost structure of setting up an industry and running it viably outweighs the incentives offered by the State. Moreover, the State did not have an industrial policy until 1982. While India's efforts towards industrialization started with the Second Plan (1956-61), the first industrial policy of the State was framed exactly after 35 years of independence and after 10 years of statehood. It is followed by three more revised policies in 1989, 1990 and 1996.

Government of Manipur initially decided that the State should act as the entrepreneur for the development of the industrial sector in Manipur (Industrial Policy of Manipur 1982). While the State is supposed to undertake the medium and large industrial projects, it will encourage small scale industries to grow under private initiative. The 1982 Policy identified bamboo based industries, starch and glucose factory, mechanised dye house, cement factory, plywood factory and sugar factory for establishment under public sector.

Weaving, sericulture, traditional handicrafts and production of various electrical goods are encouraged under the private sector. In order to accelerate the process of growth of the indigenous entrepreneurial class, the Government of Manipur committed itself to arrange industrial training to select people in these areas. In order to encourage the entrepreneurs to establish industries in Manipur, the government adopted an incentive package that include octroi relief, exemption from stamp duty and registration charges, allotment of government land at subsidised rate, government purchase, interest subsidy, exemption of sales tax, equipment subsidy and exemption of water tax (Industrial Policy of Manipur 1982).

The 1982 Policy, however, could not bear immediate fruit. The late 1980s saw the materialization of the policy as most of the public sector units came up during this period. We shall be dealing with these units later. But, the feasibility of these large and medium scale industries was questionable and it was soon realised that the small industries had more potential in the State rather than large and medium units. Thus, the government shifted its focus to small scale and agro-based industries in the 1990 Industrial Policy. Although Government of Manipur had adopted an industrial policy in 1989 but it was soon replaced without any trial in 1990.

The 1990 Policy shifted the focus from large and medium scale industries to small and agro-based industries. The main strategy of the policy was to set up small scale industries based on available local raw materials and local demand. It also focused on employment generation among the local people. As such, it identified the areas like agro-based industries, handloom and handicrafts, development of electronics, petro-chemicals based industries and forest based industries, which do not involve extensive felling of trees as priority areas. It also emphasised tourism industry as one of the promising areas of development. It was also mentioned that the State Government will urge the Central Government to establish central public sector units.

As an incentive package, the government rendered land allotment, allotment of shed to small scale industry units, manpower development, State capital investment subsidy, State transport subsidy, interest subsidy, power subsidy, subsidy on drawal of power lines, subsidy for feasibility study and project report preparation, subsidy for technical know-how, government purchase, reimbursement and exemption of local sales tax and reimbursement of stamp duty and registration fee (Industrial Policy of Manipur 1990).

It was expressly mentioned that the Industrial Policy of 1990 would be valid only for a period of five years and, thus, a new industrial policy was framed in 1996. The 1996 policy was framed keeping in mind the changing economic scenario in the post-1991 liberalization era and the post-1994 era of border trade agreement with Myanmar. The State Government decided to adopt a multi-dimensional strategy, which depends not only on subsidy/incentive regime but, which optimises the State's potential and offsets her disadvantages. In the meantime, the government realised that the developments of infrastructure as well as creation of business environment are a *sine qua non* for industrial development in the State. The Industrial Policy of 1996 emphasised on "creation of an integrated investor-friendly environment", "infrastructural development", "maximizing resource utilization", "quality improvement and skill upgradation", "revival of sick industries" and "promotion of Indo-Myanmar border trade".

The 1996 Policy sought for the establishment of a special monitoring cell to assess and provide requisite security to all major industrial investment in the State. It also sought the intervention of the Central Government in the industrialization of special category States like Manipur and urged for establishing central public sector units. To meet the infrastructural needs, the State, in addition to upgradation of facilities at Takyelpat Industrial Estate, sought to take up a phased development of Integrated Infrastructural Development Centre at Moreh in Chandel District, Export Promotion Industrial Park at Kakching in Thoubal District, Export Processing Zone at Moreh in Chandel District, Industrial Growth Centre at Kanglatongbi in Senapati District and four additional industrial locations; *viz.*, Jiribam (Imphal), Litan (Ukhrul), Noney (Tamenglong) and Nambol (Bishnupur) to catalyze balanced dispersal of industries.

The major thrust areas identified are agro-based industries, industries based on locally available raw materials, including minerals and waste, products with local/regional demand, all units, which take advantage of the Indo-Myanmar border trade, handloom and handicraft, electronics, petro-chemical based industries, forest based industries not involving depletion of the tree population, export oriented activities/industries, all non-polluting labour intensive units, units using non-conventional energy devices/systems/technology and tourism. Besides identifying new areas, the government also sought for the revival of sick industrial units by way of disinvestment and joint ventures (Industrial Policy of Manipur 1996).

In order to promote Indo-Myanmar border trade, the government sought to set up an export cell in the Directorate of Commerce and Industries, which will be the nodal agency, which will educate, train and guide traders/entrepreneurs in international trading, conduct an export potential survey, undertake measures to promote trade motivated industrial activity, optimise use of agriculture/horticulture/forest resources across the border, and facilitate setting up of trade centres with integrated and in-house basic facilities (Industrial Policy of Manipur 1996).

The government, in order to materialise the above objectives, rendered an incentive package, which includes land allotment, allotment of shed to small scale units, manpower development, State capital investment subsidy, State transport subsidy, interest subsidy, power subsidy, subsidy for feasibility study and project report preparation, subsidy for technical know-how, government purchase, reimbursement and exemption of local sales tax and reimbursement of stamp duty and registration fee, quality control and subsidy for modernization/ expansion/diversification (Industrial Policy of Manipur 1996).

Thus, we can see from the above that the strategy of the Government of Manipur towards industrialization of the State has two facets. Till 1990, the government assumed the role of an entrepreneur and tried to industrialise the State. Having failed in this objective, as we shall see later, the government after 1990 took a U-turn and bestowed the whole responsibility of industrialization of the State upon the shoulder of the people. Since 1990, the government assumed the role of a manager and focused on providing suitable business environment and industrial infrastructure. However, the absence of indigenous entrepreneurial class and with the gradual disappearance of the State from the scene, the process of industrializing Manipur has taken a backseat.

Performance of Industries

As has already been mentioned above, following the 1982 Industrial Policy, the Government of Manipur took the initiative of establishing large and medium industries. However, there is no public sector unit

Table 6.1: Public Sector Undertakings in Manipur

Sl. No.	*Name of the Units*	*Year of Incorpor-ation*	*Share Capital (₹ in Lakhs)*
1.	Manipur Agro Industries Corporation Ltd. (MAICL)	1982	200
2.	Manipur Cement Ltd. (MCL)	1988	350
3.	Manipur Cycle Corporation Ltd. (MCCL)	1985	100
4.	Manipur Electronics Development Corporation Ltd. (MANITRON)	1987	300
5.	Manipur Handloom and Handicrafts Development Corporation Ltd. (MHHDCL)	1976	40
6.	Manipur Industrial Development Corporation Ltd. (MANIDCO)	1987	1300
7.	Manipur Plantation Crops Corporation Ltd. (MPCCL)	1981	200
8.	Manipur Spinning Mills Corporation Ltd. (MSMCL)	1974	1300

Source: Government of Manipur, 1994.

worth mentioning and whatever had been established are now in the process of liquidation.

Table 6.1 gives a list of the public sector undertakings in the State. It is seen that most of the units have come up in the post-Statehood period. However, in the late 1980s, a number of units have come up. But one can see that the efforts towards industrialization in the State started after about 40 years of independence. In spite of the planned strategy of development since 1950, the State has not been able to materialise the process of industrialization until 1980s. While the India's efforts towards industrialization started with the Second Plan (1956-61), it was yet to make any headway in case of Manipur. However, one will see that even after the establishment of these units, Manipur is still an industrially backward State owing to the non-performance of these industries.

Table 6.2 gives the profit/loss, return on equity and return on investment of the public sector undertakings in Manipur in 1989, 1991 and 1993. It may be seen that most of the units are loss making units except MANITRON. It was making a profit of ₹ 20.19 lakhs, ₹ 16.55 lakhs and ₹ 21.49 lakhs in 1989, 1991 and 1993, respectively. In case of MAICL, it kept on fluctuating and though it registered a loss of ₹ 9.13 lakhs in 1991, it was making a profit of ₹ 6.17 lakhs in 1993. Though MANIDCO was making a profit of ₹ 33.65 lakhs in the initial years of establishment, it lost significance in the subsequent years and was running on a loss. However, MHHDCL was running on a loss throughout the years despite having a comparative potential in the State.

In case of return on equity, except MANITRON, all the units were making a negative return on equity. However, the return on equity in case of MANITRON also declined over the years from 33.72 per cent in 1989 to 9.59 per cent and 7.23 per cent in 1991 and 1993, respectively. MAICL also made a positive return on equity of 5.24 per cent in 1993 despite its negative return of 15.67 per cent in 1991. MANIDCO though made a positive return on equity of 7.03 per cent in 1989, it registered negative return in the subsequent years.

However, all the units made a negative return on investment. Only MAICL registered a positive return on investment of 31.11 per cent in 1993 despite making a negative return of 47.90 per cent in 1991. MANITRON, which was making profit and having a positive

Table 6.2: Performance of Public Sector Undertakings in Manipur

Name of the unit	*Profit (+)/Loss (–) (₹ Lakhs)*			*Return on equity (%)*			*Return on investment (%)*		
Year	1989	1991	1993	1989	1991	1993	1989	1991	1993
MAICL	0.82	–9.13	6.17	2.62	–15.67	5.24	6.67	–47.9	31.11
MCL	0	–40.65	–37.5	0	–10.79	–11.36	0	–11.15	–11.01
MCCL	–7.49	–6.33	–5.67	–22.52	–28.21	–36.94	–29.25	–32.28	–38.21
MANITRON	20.19	16.55	21.49	33.72	9.59	7.23	–153.89	–100.24	–50.8
MHHDCL	–37.65	–22.54	–39.88	–20.54	–11.66	–70.28	–18.44	–58.93	–107.73
MANIDCO	33.65	–100.59	–36.18	7.03	–8.29	–2.5	30.31	–50.43	–17.71
MPCCL	–186.89	–18.54	–18.58	–77.5	–4.94	–4.06	–91.55	–7.89	–6.05
MSMCL	–159.79	–95.07	–172.98	–25.14	–12.35	–18.42	–52.5	–39.59	–87.67

Source: Government of Manipur, 1994.

return on equity throughout the years, however, registered a negative return on investment to the tune of 153.89 per cent, 100.24 per cent and 50.80 per cent in 1989, 1991 and 1993, respectively. MANIDCO, which was making a positive return on investment of 30.31 per cent in 1989 registered negative return of 50.43 per cent and 17.71 per cent in 1991 and 1993, respectively.

Thus, we see that the public sector undertakings are not viable and all are making losses. All the units registered a negative return on equity and on investment. On account of the non-performance of these units, the government has taken up steps of winding up the sick units. According to the Annual Administrative Report (2008-09) of the Directorate of Commerce and Industries, all the units are in active process of winding up except MANITRON, MANIDCO and MHHDCL. All the staffs of the units, which are under the process of winding up had already been retrenched, except 12 employees were retained to complete the updating of accounts of these units. With the failure of the State in her efforts to industrialise the State by setting up large and medium scale industries, the government focused on small scale industries from 1990. Let us now see the performance of the small scale industries.

Table 6.3 gives the growth of small scale industries in Manipur. The number of small scale units increased from 6,319 in 1990 to 9,415 and 9,690 in 2000 and 2007 (upto 31-03-2007), respectively. So, in about 17 years time the small scale units grew at the rate of about more than 50 per cent. However, the average number of employment per unit is around five persons and the average investment in plant and machinery is around ₹ 40,000. Similarly, the production per unit is below ₹ 2 lakh. But there is an increasing trend in all the parameters from 1990 to 2007. The average number of employment increased from 4.98 persons in 1990 to 5.15 persons and 5.35 persons in 2000 and 2007, respectively. The average investment in plant and machinery increased from ₹ 30.38 thousand in 1990 to ₹ 35.25 thousand and ₹ 41.19 thousand in 2000 and 2007, respectively. Similarly, the average production per unit increased from ₹ 1.41 lakh in 1990 to ₹ 1.60 lakh and ₹ 1.76 lakh in 2000 and 2007, respectively.

From the above observation one can deduce the nature of small scale industries in Manipur. It appears that the small scale industries in Manipur are more or less demand based units, which are operating

Table 6.3: Growth of Small Scale Industrial Units (both SIDO and Non-SIDO) in Manipur

Year	*No. of units*	*No. of employment*	*Average no. of employment per unit*	*Investment in plant and machinery (Rs. Crore)*	*Average investment per unit (Rs. Thousand)*	*Production (Rs. Crore)*	*Average production per unit (Rs. lakh)*
1990	6319	31500	4.98	19.2	30.38	89.11	1.41
2000	9415	48514	5.15	33.19	35.25	150.69	1.6
2007*	9690	51829	5.35	39.91	41.19	170.77	1.76

Source: Government of Manipur 2004. (*Upto 31-03-2007).

at household level. There is no huge employment or huge investment. Even the productions in these units are not very high. These are basically need-based industries, which are run by a few people and are somewhat more or less subsistence in nature. No doubt, these are important agents of an economy but they will not be in a position to lift Manipur to the level of a developed industrial state.

The Khadi and Village Industry (KVI) is also another category where traditional small industries are grouped. In Manipur, the KVI was constituted in the year 1966 following the establishment of KVI Commission by the Government of India in the year 1957.

Table 6.4: Performance of Khadi and Village Industries in Manipur

Item	*1998*	*1999*	*Growth rate (1998-99)*	*2003*	*2004*	*Growth rate (2003-04)*
Production (₹ Lakh)	2978.57	4457.27	49.64	6000.85	6029.24	0.47
Sales (₹ Lakh)	3151.84	4602.41	46.02	5661.92	6069.88	7.21
Earnings (₹ Lakh)	962.13	1385.01	43.95	2632.68	2690.18	2.18
Employment (₹ Lakh)	0.42	0.42	—	0.61	0.62	1.64

Source: Government of Manipur 2004 and Government of India 2006.

Table 6.4 gives the performance of the Khadi and Village industries in Manipur. During the late 1990s, the production was growing at a rate of around 50 per cent. This has declined to less than one per cent in 2003-2004. The sales, which were growing at a rate of around 46 per cent during 1998-1999, declined to about seven per cent in 2003-2004. Similarly, the earning of the KVI, which was growing around 43 per cent in 1998-1999, declined to about two per cent in 2003-2004. However, the employment has increased during 2003-2004 and is growing at the rate less than 2 per cent. The KVI is, thus, facing a retrogressive change.

Given the above nature of industries in Manipur, we may safely conclude that the secondary sector in the State is basically non-agricultural activities of very low scale. The Economic Census gives an idea of non-agricultural activities of the State.

Table 6.5: Number of Enterprises and Workers according to Economic Census

Economic census	*Agricultural enterprises*					*Non-Agricultural enterprises*				
	Rural	*Urban*	*Total*	*Persons usually working*	*Hired workers*	*Rural*	*Urban*	*Total*	*Persons usually working*	*Hired workers*
1980	1765	552	2417	4839	360	17097	15231	32328	100120	55355
1990	3787	1190	4977	9701	548	30034	26253	56287	147667	75972
1998	4235	1938	6173	12867	1017	38785	35531	74316	187859	102904
2002	5751	2542	8293	14509	1823	51830	44609	96439	221567	90030
1980-2005 Growth Rate (%)								198.31	121.3	62.64

Source: Government of Manipur, 2001, 2002 and 2008.

Table 6.5 shows that the non-agricultural enterprises increased from 32,328 in 1980 to 56,287 and 74,316 in 1990 and 1998, respectively. So, in 25 years time the non-agricultural enterprises have grown by about 198 per cent. The number of persons usually employed in these enterprises has increased from 100,120 persons in 1980 to 221,567 persons in 2005. The employment in these enterprises has grown by about 121 per cent in 25 years. In case of hired workers, it has increased from 55,355 persons in 1980 to 90,030 persons in 2005, registering a growth of about 62 per cent. One can observe that the growth of number of enterprises outweighs the growth in employment. Moreover, the average number of persons working in these enterprises was about three persons per enterprise in 1980. But in the Census of 1990, 1998 and 2005, the average number of persons employed was less than three persons per enterprise. In case of hired workers, the average was less than two persons per enterprise throughout the census years.

Contribution to the Economy

As is expected of such low performance of industries, the contribution of secondary sector to the total income of the State is also low. From Table 6.6, it can be discerned that the share of secondary sector to total Net State Domestic Product (NSDP) in Manipur has increased over the years. While the share was very low to the tune of 10.28 per

Table 6.6: Contribution of Secondary Sector to Total NSDP in Manipur (% share)

Year	*Manufacturing*			*Construction*	*Electricity, gas and water supply*	*Total secondary*
	Regd.	*Unregd.*	*Total*			
1961	—	—	—	1.68	0.25	10.28
1970	—	—	—	1.89	0.4	8.86
1980	0.48	6.24	6.72	11.67	–0.23	18.16
1990	0.08	5.68	5.76	7.91	–4.18	9.48
2000	0.06	8.2	8.26	11.54	0.31	20.12
2007	0.15	5.88	6.03	23.26	1.73	31.11
2008	0.16	5.8	5.96	24.34	1.69	31.99
2009	0.16	5.71	5.87	25.39	1.6	32.87

Source: Calculated from EPW and CSO.

cent and 8.86 per cent in 1961 and 1970, respectively, it has increased to 18.16 per cent in 1980. However, its share declined to 9.48 per cent in 1990. Since then, the share of secondary sector has increased and its share was 20.12 per cent and 31.11 per cent in 2000 and 2007, respectively, thus becoming the major contributor to the State's income. In 2008 and 2009 the share was 31.99 per cent and 32.87 per cent, respectively.

Table 6.7: Percentage Share of Various Components in Secondary Sector in Manipur

Year	Manufacturing			Construction	Electricity, gas and water supply
	Regd.	Unregd.	Total		
1961	—	—	—	16.36	2.46
1970	—	—	—	21.35	4.49
1980	2.65	34.35	37	64.29	–1.28
1990	0.85	59.85	60.7	83.41	44.1
2000	0.29	40.77	41.06	57.38	1.57
2007	0.48	18.95	19.43	74.98	5.58
2008	0.5	18.13	18.63	76.09	5.28
2009	0.5	17.39	17.89	77.26	4.86

Source: Calculated from EPW and CSO.

However, a further break-up of the components of the secondary sector will give us a true picture of the nature of growth in this sector (see Table 6.7). In the secondary sector construction is the leading activity. Though its share before 1970 was very insignificant, contributing around 20 per cent, it has been the major activity of growth after 1970s. Its share, which was 64.29 per cent in 1980 increased to 83.41 per cent in 1990. However, the share declined to 57.38 per cent in 2000 but improved to 74.98 per cent in 2007. Its share was 76.09 per cent and 77.26 per cent in 2008 and 2009, respectively.

The manufacturing unit whose share was more than 70 per cent before 1970 lost its significance. Its share, which stood at 81.15 per cent and 74.16 per cent in 1961 and 1970, respectively declined to 60 per cent in 1980. Since then its share has been declining and its share stood at 41.06 per cent in 2000. It has further declined to 19.43 per cent in 2007. In 2008 and 2009 its share further declined to 18.63 per cent and 17.89 per cent, respectively.

A very interesting observation within the secondary sector is that the share of registered manufacturing unit is insignificant. Its share varied between one per cent and two per cent over the years. Since 1990 its share has dropped below one per cent. Major contribution to manufacturing comes from unregistered units. Same is the case with electricity, gas and water supply. Its share, which stood once at 4.49 per cent in 1970, has gone negative to the tune of –44.10 per cent in 1990. But it has shown some sign of improvement in the preceding years and contributed 1.57 per cent and 5.58 per cent in 2000 and 2007, respectively. But its share has declined recently to 5.28 per cent and 4.86 per cent in 2007 and 2008, respectively.

Table 6.8: Distribution of Main Workers by Industries in Secondary Sector in Manipur (% Share)

Classification	*1961*	*1971*	*1981*	*1991*	*2001**
Mining and quarrying	0	0.02	0.04	0.03	NA
Manufacturing, processing, servicing and repairing in household industry	22.12	9.34	9.68	5.8	6.55
Manufacturing, processing, servicing and repairing other than household industry	0.31	1.65	1.8	2.31	NA
Construction	0.62	1.25	1.88	1.55	NA
Total Secondary	**23.05**	**12.23**	**13.35**	**9.66**	**6.55**

Source: Government of Manipur 2006.

* Figures for 2001 exclude Mao-Maram, Paomata and Purul Sub-divisions of Senapati District.

Though the share to the total income of the State keeps on fluctuating, the share of working population in this sector is declining. The share of main workers in the secondary sector as a whole declined from 23.05 per cent in 1961 to 12.23 per cent in 1971. It slightly increased to 13.35 per cent in 1981. Since then it declined to 9.66 per cent and 6.55 per cent in 1991 and 2001, respectively (see Table 6.8).

A major portion of the working population in secondary sector is engaged in manufacturing, processing, servicing and repairing in household industry. It may be noted that in 1961, the share of main workers engaged in manufacturing, processing, servicing and repairing in household industry accounts for 22.12 per cent. But in the following years it declined to 9.34 per cent and 9.68 per cent in

1971 and 1981, respectively. It further declined to 5.80 per cent and 6.55 per cent in 1991 and 2001, respectively. The main reason for a high percentage share in 1961 is that in the Census of 1961, subsidiary activities like weaving was included in this category, which was subsequently dropped in the following census (IDBI 1972, 5). The share of main workers engaged in manufacturing, processing, servicing and repairing other than household industry gradually increased from 0.31 per cent in 1961 to 1.65 per cent, 1.80 per cent and 2.31 per cent in 1971, 1981 and 1991, respectively. Similarly, the share of main workers engaged in construction increased from 0.62 per cent in 1961 to 1.25 per cent, 1.88 per cent and 1.55 per cent in 1971, 1981 and 1991, respectively. However, the share of main workers engaged in mining and quarrying is very low and negligible, less than 0.5 per cent over the census years.

Conclusion

The above analysis shows that the industrial sector in Manipur is, in fact, in doldrums. The increasing share of secondary sector to total NSDP is because of construction activities and there is hardly any industry whose share is worth mentioning. Moreover, the non-agricultural enterprises are also basically household based enterprises and they are neither labour nor capital intensive. Considering the above features, Amar Yumnam has rightly pointed out that there is absence of externalities in the non-agricultural enterprises in the State (Yumnam 2005, 93).

The backwardness of the industrial sector in the State, however, can also be attributed to non-availability of core natural resources, geographical isolation leading to high transport cost, topography, paucity of infrastructural facilities, limited size of the local market, *etc.* In addition, the meagre amount of plan spending over the years and the policies towards industrialization has failed to provide a "big push", which is very much needed for an underdeveloped economy. While the State also called for Lewis type transformation, the surplus agricultural labour did not find a place due to weak industrial base, which is very much required for any agrarian economy to transform itself. As there exists a close relationship between industrial growth, productivity growth and Gross Domestic Product growth, developing a strong industrial base is key towards overall growth and development of the State.

Increasing the share of plan spending towards industries is the first and foremost step towards industrialization in the State. As setting up industries and success of the same calls for heavy investment in social overhead capital, this sector should be developed side by side along with the industries. The industries to be set up should be such that they have a strong dyadic linkage with the local resources available. Creating a strong resource-industry linkage will help sustain the industries in the long run for a land-locked State like Manipur. As such, agriculture and horticulture based industries should be given top priority. Handloom, handicrafts, cane and bamboo based industries are the next in line, which have a strong potential in the State. As far as minerals are concerned, limestone, serpentinite and idocrase have been reported to be found in Ukhrul and Chandel districts. As of now these resources are unutilised and steps towards proper utilization of these resources should be taken up. In order that the dream towards industrialization of the State is fulfilled, creating an investor friendly environment is a must as setting up industries and success of the same calls for huge investment not only from the government but also from private individuals. An investor friendly environment will boost up business confidence, which in turn will attract investment, which will lead to successful operation and long-term sustenance of the industrial sector in the State.

REFERENCES

Central Statistical Organization (CSO). www.mospi.nic.in.

Economic and Political Weekly Research Foundation. (2003). *Domestic Product of States of India 1960-61 to 2000-01*. Mumbai.

Government of India. (2006). *Basic Statistics of North Eastern Region 2006.* Shillong: North Eastern Council.

Government of Manipur. *Industrial Policy of Manipur 1982, 1989, 1990 and 1996.* Imphal: Directorate of Commerce and Industries.

_______. (1994). *An Analysis of the Performance of the State Public Sector Undertakings 1988-1993.* Imphal: Planning Department.

_______. (2001). *Fourth Economic Census 1998 Manipur*. Imphal: Directorate of Economics and Statistics.

_______. (2002). *Statistical Handbook of Manipur 2002.* Imphal: Directorate of Economics and Statistics.

Government of Manipur. (2004). *Economic Survey Manipur 2002-03*. Imphal: Directorate of Economics and Statistics.

_______. (2006). *Statistical Abstract Manipur 2005*. Imphal: Directorate of Economics and Statistics.

_______. (2008). *Fifth Economic Census 2005 Manipur*. Imphal: Directorate of Economics and Statistics.

_______. (2009). *Annual Administrative Report 2008-2009*. Imphal: Directorate of Commerce and Industries.

Industrial Development Bank of India (IDBI). (1972). *Industrial Potential Survey Manipur.* Bombay.

Singh, K. Gyanendra. (2011). *Security and Development: The Political Economy of Insurgency in Manipur*. New Delhi: Akansha Publishing House.

Yumnam, Amar. (2005). Development experience of Manipur: A framework for industrialization. In *Structural Change and Strategy of Development: Resource-Industry Linkages in North-East India*, edited by Gurudas Das. New Delhi: Akansha Publishing House.

7

Employment Structure of Agricultural Labourers in Manipur

Silvia Lisam

The paper attempts a comparative analysis of employment structure of agricultural labourers in two villages of Manipur. Essentially, the present study attempts to capture the variation in the employment structure of a village situated close to urban centre as compared to a village located far from the urban centre. Our findings show how in the face of scarcity of on-farm employment in an agrarian village, off-farm employment provide some support to the livelihoods of these agricultural labour families. The paper explains the way in which agricultural labourers allocate employment under different sets of conditions the way they combine different categories of economic activities.

Introduction

The study is based on a survey of two villages from two valley districts of Manipur. It was considered appropriate to select a village from a region closely connected to the urban centre and the other village from a region far from the urban centre in order to give a comparative picture on employment structure of agricultural labour.

The first village under study (Taobungkhok) is situated at about eight kilometres away from Imphal under Patsoi assembly constituency of Imphal West district. The village is located at about a mile's distance from the New Cachar road on the south of the Langjing hilllock. The entire village is surrounded by paddy fields. There is one inter-village road connecting New Cachar Road and Tiddim Road passing through the Taobungkhok village. The settlement area of the village is divided into three segments such as Awang Leikai, Mayai Leikai and Makha Leikai. There are only two government primary schools located within the village and also two English medium schools are seen to have emerged near the village. Each locality (*leikai*) has a local club with office bearers from the respective *leikai* for the purpose of developmental activities in the village and to share the grievances of the villagers. As such, there is no big market within the village but few vegetable vendors are seen in each courtyard of the respective clubs. There are three to four grocery shops in each *leikai*.

The second village that we have chosen for field survey, Tejpur, is a new village located at about 45 kms. away from Imphal under the Hiyanglam constituency of Thoubal District. The village is situated at about 2 km. from the state highway adjacent to Wabagai Bazar. The settlement area is divided into three segments namely Awang Leikai, Mayai Leikai and Makha Leikai. Since the area coverage of Tejpur is smaller than that of Taobungkhok, there are two local clubs and one primary school. As such, there is no specific market in the village but the villagers reported that most of them go out to the main market of Wabagai or Kakching to meet their requirements. Each *leikai* has only one grocery shop. Contrary to Taobungkhok, not a single vegetable vendor could be seen in Tejpur.

Information was collected in three rounds of survey. The main purpose of the first round was to identify the village and get acquainted with the villagers. Instead of structured questionnaire, informal conversation was used to get the required information. In the second round of survey, a census of households was conducted to collect general information like demographic and educational profile, economic profile, occupational profile as well as debt profile. The total number of household in Taobungkhok and Tejpur are 419 and 174, respectively.

In the third round of survey, a labour schedule was used, in which information of number of days of employment of the labour households in on-farm sector, off-farm sector and self-employment were recorded. A sample of 50 labour households (landless as well as land-owning) were selected from Tejpur village. All landless labour households (39 households) were selected and the rest (11 households) were selected on the basis of stratified random sampling from among the marginal land holders. For Taobungkhok, all landless households consisting of 50 households were selected and the rest 23 households were selected on the basis of stratified random sampling from among the marginal landholders.

Macro Picture of Occupational Structure

Employment of the rural labour is determined by the levels of development both in the farm and non-farm sectors within the rural context and the generation of employment in the urban centres in conjunction with the degrees of mobility of the rural work force. Our finding shows that both the villages use mono-crop paddy and high levels of modern inputs. Tejpur village widely practices cash cropping whereas it is an exception in Taobungkhok village. On the other hand, Taobungkhok has a much larger growth in the non-farm sector. Again, Taobungkhok village feeds the much larger demand for wage labour and other regular employment demands of the capital town of the State whereas Tejpur village feeds the demands of a much smaller town of Kakching. These structural as well as economic geography differentials are starkly reflected in the occupational structure of heads of households in the two villages as has been found out from our census survey.

The biggest share of occupation in Taobungkhok village comprises of government service as well as private sector employee (40%) for heads of households. But in the case of Tejpur, cultivators and agricultural labourers are the leading occupation in the village. Even though, Taobungkhok is an agrarian village, high level of occupational diversification from farm sector to non-farm sector has taken place. In the village and household heads cultivation as their main source of income is very low but the percentage of agricultural labour shows that people dependent on agriculture still persists. There are still 94 heads of households (about 23%) in the village who claim agricultural labour as their subsidiary occupation. They rely on multiple occupations to support their livelihood. The same figure also indicates that probably these people have shifted to non-farm activities and as a result, agricultural labour has become a secondary occupation for them.

In Tejpur, there are 70 household heads (about 40%) claiming cultivation as their main source of livelihood and 50 households (about 29%) as agricultural laborer. Therefore, cultivators and agricultural labour together constituted about 69 per cent in the occupational structure of the total households. There are only three household heads who are government employees. The location of this village forced the people to confine to agricultural activities and in the absence of alternative employment opportunities, these people had to depend on agriculture to support their livelihoods. On the other hand, the village of Taobungkhok exhibits symptoms of the non-viability of agriculture as reflected in the occupational structure with a high proportion of the household heads claiming to have engaged in the secondary and tertiary sector activities and an insignificant proportion of population are engaged in agricultural activities as the main source of livelihoods. Scarcity of land, lack of irrigation, emerging new job opportunities, nearness to the urban centre of Imphal and high levels of education seems to have accelerated the levels of occupational diversification and pushed agricultural activities to a secondary level of livelihood options. This macro picture gives us an indication that the occupational structure is greatly influenced by their geographical locations.

Findings of the Study: Micro Level Analysis

For the purpose of the study, the distribution of occupation of agricultural labourers in the villages have been categorised into three: on-farm, off-farm and self-employment. The average days of employment of each labour were calculated in order to see the nature of employment of these labourers in each category.

Table 7.1 shows that heads of labour households are more or less fully employed in Taobungkhok village. Out of about 308 days of employment in a year, off-farm employment accounts for about 79 per cent, on-farm for about 14 per cent and self-employment for about 8 per cent. This raises the fundamental theoretical question of who an agricultural labour is. By time allocation criteria or income accrued yardstick, our sample households are seemingly or clearly not agricultural labour households. These households were identified in our census survey on the basis of the respondents' answer to the

Table 7.1: Average Number of Employment for Heads of Labour Households (excluding Non-workers) Taobungkhok

Months	*On farm*	*Self-Employment*	*Off-Farm*	*Total*
April	6.7	2.1	1.4	10.2
May	16.9	2.6	1.9	21.4
June	12.1	3.3	2.9	18.3
July	4	6	6.4	16.4
August	3.5	7.9	8.5	19.9
September	2.8	7.2	7.5	17.5
October	5.6	6.5	4	16.1
November	29	0	0	29
December	29	0	0	29
January	3.5	4.2	8	15.7
February	2.8	5.6	10.8	19.2
March	2.8	7	9.1	18.9
Total	120.7	52.4	60.5	233.6

Source: Sample Survey.

question on their main occupations in terms of time allocation. In the sample survey, when the anomaly was pointed out, all the households vehemently pleaded that they be categorised as *Lou suba* or agricultural labour as that was how they were socially categorised in the village.

They further pointed out that off-farm employment consisted of all sorts of odd jobs ranging from carpentry hands, masonry, *kutcha* house construction, earth work like *bunding*, land levelling, ditch or drain digging, loading and unloading of bricks in the brick fields, stacking of raw bricks and a host of odd manual jobs in and outside the village. Splitting up time allocation among these multifarious unskilled wage labours would result in time allocation per job category that was lower than that of about 43 days in agricultural labour in a calendar year. Thus, if agricultural labour did 10 other odd jobs for 30 days each, the total days would be 300 days though job-wise allotment of 30 days are much lower than the 42 days of agricultural labour.

For the purpose of our study, the significant issue at hand is how cultural norms enter into the dynamics of rural society, how socio-psychological parameters shape various agrarian and economic relationships and how socio-cultural branding (castes in India) infringes on economic rationale. In the villages of Taobungkhok, self-employment of heads of labour households essentially meant vegiculture on limited homestead land for family consumption and on-farm employment meant pure agricultural wage labour on one crop of paddy annually.

In Tejpur, however, we get a more representative picture of employment structures in the rural areas of the valley of Manipur. In Table 7.2, we observe that heads of labour households are employed for about 234 days in a year (about 8 months) as against 307 days (10 months) in Taobungkhok, a differential of about three months. Of the annual employment days, about 52 per cent are on-farm, about 26 per cent on off-farm and about 22 per cent on self-employment. Self-employment consists mainly of homestead cash cropping and peripheral household handicraft.

Table 7.2: Average Number of Employment for Heads of Labour Households (excluding Non-workers) Tejpur

Months	*On farm*	*Self-Employment*	*Off-Farm*	*Total*
April	0.34	2.1	23.8	26.24
May	2.1	2.1	21.7	25.9
June	2.1	1.7	22.1	25.9
July	0	1.4	23.8	25.2
August	0	2.1	23.8	25.9
September	0	2.1	23.4	25.5
October	8.6	1.4	10.7	20.7
November	29.3	0	0	29.3
December	0.5	1.7	20.3	22.5
January	0	2.8	23.8	26.6
February	0	3.1	23.8	26.9
March	0	3.1	23.8	26.9
Total	42.94	23.6	241	307.54

Source: Sample Survey.

On-farm employment in Tejpur includes employment outside the village mainly as gang labour. Off-farm employment includes carpentry, masonry, food processing, shop keeping and various odd jobs in Taobungkhok village. The non-farm sector is small in Tejpur and urban employment is limited. Thus, agricultural wage labour along with non-wage agricultural self-employment provides for about 74 per cent of employment of agricultural labour households in Tejpur village.

Table 7.3, 7.4, 7.5 and 7.6 shows that working male members of the labour householdsare similarly employed for about 240 days in Taobungkhok (21% in on-farm, 76% in off-farm and 3% of self-employment) and about 234 days in Tejpur (39% in on-farm, 24% in off-farm and 37% of self-employment).

Table 7.3: Average Number of Employment for Female Members (excluding Non-workers) Taobungkhok

Months	*On farm*	*Self-Employment*	*Off-Farm*	*Total*
April	1.1	9.5	6.1	16.7
May	23.5	0.7	1.5	25.7
June	24.1	0.6	1.5	26.2
July	9	6.5	4.6	20.1
August	0	9.2	6.8	16
September	0	10.2	6.8	17
October	4.6	6.4	3.5	14.5
November	25.4	0	0	25.4
December	2.8	4.2	7.7	14.7
January	0	12.6	7.9	20.5
February	0	12.2	7.9	20.1
March	0	12.2	7.9	20.1
Total	90.5	84.3	62.2	237

Source: Sample Survey.

Female members are employed for 237 days in Taobungkhok (38% in on-farm, 26% in off-farm and 36% of self-employment) and for about 223 days in Tejpur (38% in on-farm, 24% in off-farm and 39% of self-employment). Of the children (sons and daughters) in the households, 33 per cent in Taobungkhok and 30 per cent in Tejpur are active workers. On an average, roughly three persons in an agricultural labour household are wage worker.

It has also been observed that in both the villages surveyed, there has been a high level of female employment in on-farm activities. This high level of female employment in on-farm activities is associated with the socio-cultural and socio-economic factors prevalent in the regions. As per gender division of work in rice cultivation, transplanting is largely a female task. Weeding is another

Table 7.4: Average Number of Employment for Female Members (excluding Non-workers) Tejpur

Months	*On farm*	*Self-Employment*	*Off-Farm*	*Total*
April	1.53	3.6	5.6	10.73
May	18.2	2	3.1	23.3
June	17.5	3.1	3.6	24.2
July	0	8.1	5.1	13.2
August	0	9.2	5.6	14.8
September	0	9.5	5.1	14.6
October	0.8	9.7	2	12.5
November	23	1.5	2.5	27
December	23.4	4.1	2.5	30
January	0	12.2	6.6	18.8
February	0	11.7	5.6	17.3
March	0	11.2	5.1	16.3
Total	84.43	85.9	52.4	222.73

Source: Sample Survey.

operation that affords work for women. This is done for a month after transplanting and a woman worker can expect some days of work each weeding cycle. However, the number of person days would depend on the growth of weeds in the field. The task of harvesting, thrashing and winnowing are done by both men and women. There is a high level of male labour employment in both the village mainly during the peak harvesting season. Such a phenomenon of increasing feminisation of agricultural employment has also been observed in India in the post-green revolution era. This is because most of the activities to be performed by men have been substituted by machines.

An analysis of the employment of human labour for Maharashtra and Assam for the years 1967-68 and 1970-71 also found that in agricultural operations like harvesting, inter-culture and transplanting, female labour is preferred by employers on account of the very nature of work; and secondly, female hired labour is preferred by employers to male hired labour for certain operations in those regions where cultivation is highly non-mechanised (Chattopadhyay 1982, 46-7). Venkateshwaran pointed out that operations performed by men were substitutes for hydraulic, mechanical or electrical energy. Women almost always relied on manual labour using only their own energy. For example, transplanting and weeding require women to bend the

Table 7.5: Average Number of Employment for Male Members (excluding Non-Workers) Taobungkhok

Months	*On-farm*	*Self-employment*	*Off-farm*	*Total*
April	0.4	0	13.8	14.2
May	12.1	0	13.8	25.9
June	2.9	0	15	17.9
July	0	0	15	15
August	0	0	15	15
September	0	0	13.8	13.8
October	3.5	0	13.8	17.3
November	16	0	13.8	29.8
December	14.8	0	13.8	28.6
January	0	2.5	16.3	18.8
February	0	2.5	16.3	18.8
March	0	2.5	16.3	18.8
Total	49.7	7.5	176.7	233.9

Source: Sample Survey.

whole day and work in muddy soil with their hands (Venkateswaran1995, 24-5). This phenomenon of gender-based division of labour in some agricultural operations was found in the villages of Bihar also (Jha 1997, 160). Similarly, Aziz also pointed out that the nature of rural labour market is such that it does not hold out good prospects for agricultural labourers. It is characterised by highly seasonal employment and attracts a substantial number of women and children and the owner cultivator group (Aziz 1984, 36). A study in an agriculturally developed village in Kheda district of Gujarat also shows a declining trend in the male worker population ratio but a significant rise in the female worker population ratio (Kumar1996, 815). Therefore, the low income households provide disproportionately large number of women into the rural labour force.

When we look into the picture of self-employment of male agricultural labour in Taobungkhok, an important phenomenon of massive occupational diversification into non-farm sector has been observed that is, the average days of self-employment for these male labourers is almost nil throughout the calendar year. The days of self-employment is about eight for the male labourers. Male labourers in Taobungkhok often move out of the village in search of employment in the urban areas during lean season. When we see the picture of

Table 7.6: Average Number of Employment for Male Members (excluding Non-workers) Tejpur

Months	*On-farm*	*Self-employment*	*Off-farm*	*Total*
April	0	11.8	7.1	18.9
May	23.7	0	0.8	24.5
June	22.1	0	0.8	22.9
July	1.6	10.7	5.3	17.6
August	0	7.4	5.5	12.9
September	0	9.5	5.5	15
October	4.7	5.5	2.6	12.8
November	26.7	0	0	26.7
December	12.6	3.2	4.7	20.5
January	0	13.2	7.9	21.1
February	0	12.4	7.9	20.3
March	0	12.4	7.9	20.3
Total	91.4	86.1	56	233.5

Source: Sample Survey.

employment days in off-farm employment, the average days of off-farm employment is about 177.

Thus, off-farm sector plays important role in providing employment even in the peak harvesting season of November. This shows the declining importance of on-farm employment in Taobungkhok and greater occupational diversification is taking place because of its close connectivity with the urban centre. An interesting picture observed is that of all the three categories of employment in Taobungkhok, that is, off-farm, on-farm and self-employment, these male labourers get highest average days of employment in off-farm activities. Looking at the picture of occupational structure of male agricultural labour in Tejpur, it is observed that the supply of agricultural labour is more in Tejpur, that is, people willing to work as agricultural labour is more in Tejpur as compared to Taobungkhok. A possible reason for this high level of employment in Tejpur is that there is less availability of non-farm job in and around the village. As has been mentioned earlier, the village being situated far from the urban centre, moving out of the village in search of non-farm employment is not so easy. For daily commuting to the city, it takes a longer time as compared to Taobungkhok. Moreover, these labourers cannot get assured employment throughout the year. When we see the picture of self-employment, we found that the average days of self-employment in Tejpur for male labourer is quite high which is quite contrary to the case that we have observed in the case of Taobungkhok.

This phenomenon of some sections of rural workers reporting non-agricultural employment in nearby urban areas but residing in the village depends on the proximity to urban centres, the size of the urban centre relative to the rural population of the area, the case of access to transport and the costs of commuting. The larger the nearby town, shorter the commuting distance and cheaper the cost is, larger is likely to be the incidence of this phenomenon.

Findings of the Study: Macro Level Analysis

Table 7.7 and 7.8 shows that households in Taobungkhok are able to get employment for about 439 days in a year as compared to 462 days in Tejpur. This employment differential is accounted for by the far higher degrees of self-employment in Tejpur village along with larger on-farm employment. The percentage distribution of sectoral employment shows that about 30, 52 and 18 per cent are the respective shares for on-farm, off-farm and self-employment in Taobungkhok. In Tejpur village, the percentage distribution is about 34, 26 and 41 for on-farm, off-farm and self-employment, respectively. It is evident that household employment structure is heavily weighed in favour of

Table 7.7: Distribution of Employment Availability per Labour Household into On-farm, Off-farm and Self-employment within and Outside the Village (Taobungkhok)

Category	*Male*			*Female*			*Total*
	In	*Out*	*Total*	*In*	*Out*	*Total*	
No. of person days per household (on farm)	50.3	0	50.3	80.3	0	80.3	130.6 (29.76)
No. of person days per household (off farm)	70.1	90.2	160.3	36.1	32.1	68.2	228.5 (52.07)
No. of person days per household (self employment)	8.7	0	8.7	71	0	71	79.7 (18.16)
Total	**129.1**	**90.2**	**219.3**	**187.4**	**32.1**	**219.5**	**438.8**

Source: Sample Survey.

Table 7.8: Distribution of Employment Availability Per Labour Household into On-farm, Off-farm and Self-employment within and Outside the Village (Tejpur)

Category	Male			Female			Total
	In	Out	Total	In	Out	Total	
No. of person days per household (on farm)	46.3	32.2	78.5	51.3	26.7	78	156.5 (33.84)
No. of person days per household (off farm)	33.4	36	69.4	18.1	30.1	48.2	117.6 (25.5)
No. of person days per household (self emp.)	82.5	0	82.5	105.4	0	105.4	187.9 (40.76)
Total	**162.2**	**68.2**	**230.4**	**174.8**	**56.8**	**231.6**	**462**

Source: Sample Survey.

off-farm economic activities in Taobungkhok Village (about 52%) and more weighed in favour of agricultural self-employment in Tejpur Village (about 41%). Dependence on agriculture (paddy cultivation) for both the villages are low. It is about 30 per cent in Taobungkhok and 34 in Tejpur.

The level of development of transport network, as well as size and density of village settlements would seem to be relevant in determining the location, organisation and hence, labour intensity of non-agricultural activities. It seems more likely in situation where commercialisation has advanced and the wage labour system has become widespread in as much as both tend to weaken the traditional social mechanisms for taking care of the unemployed/underemployed and increases the pressure on those who cannot find work in agriculture to seek other avenues of employment. And in terms of the conventional demand-supply analysis of labour market, if the absorptive capacity of agriculture and urban areas is limited, the pressure of excess labour supply in rural areas will fall more heavily on rural non-agricultural sector which means that the level of rural non-agricultural wage rate relative to the agricultural wage should be quite sensitive to the extent of imbalance between labour supply and demand in rural areas (Vaidyanathan 1986, 131). Thus, the higher the rate of unemployment, the higher is likely to be the share of rural non-agricultural sector in total rural employment and the lower the non-agricultural wage relative to that of agriculture.

The Indian labour market is complicated, more so in the rural economy. Much has been argued about how a simple demand and supply model cannot capture this complexity. "Labour is controlled not only through the manipulation of various non-class social identities but also through the segmentation and fragmentation of labour markets" (White 2004, 20). Caste still shapes the ideologies of work and status in India. In other words, workers themselves sometimes enforce the stratification of occupation by castes so as to maintain their hold over enclaves of the labour market or sectors of petty trade. It was found in Bihar that almost half of the agriculture labours are from the scheduled castes, the rest mainly comprises of scheduled tribes and other backward castes (Singh and Kumar 1993, 998). These social identities still affect the types of work done and more importantly the terms and conditions of labour contracts. A recent study in West Bengal found that there were as many as twelve types of labour contracts and there are no single village wages for casual labour (White 2004, 21), labour contracts being affected by gender, caste and age.

In Manipur, the labour market is segmented and fragmented on lines of gender and age but not on caste lines, being essentially a casteless society. With fixity of cropped area in the small valley region, slow pace of growth of the non-farm sector in the rural areas and non-industrialisation in the State's economy, the ever growing mass of wage labour are constantly circulating village to village or village to town in search of wage labour. Rural on-farm employment is essentially seasonal in character, and therefore, they overworked mainly during sowing and harvesting season (Singh 2010, 54). Rural agricultural labour find on-farm employment for hardly three months in a year spread over the mono crop cycle during June and November. As such, all agricultural labour households adopt a diversified strategy of labour supplies to ensure maximum annual employment. Under such fragmented demand and supply conditions, labour contracts are oral and customary and no written contracts are entered into. In the agrarian sector, some degree of labour tying is prevalent in the form of wage advances to labour for assured labour during peak agricultural cycles. In our villages, we found that an advance of ₹ 50 was paid in off season for work during peak season when daily wages would be

₹ 80. However, the incidence of such labour relations is mainly confined among the landless labourer and on a small scale.

Conclusion

Our analysis shows that the employment structure is different in the two villages. In Taobungkhok, a high level of occupational diversification from farm to non-farm sector is taking place as reflected in our findings whereas in Tejpur, the non-farm sector is small and the scope of urban employment in the nearby town is limited as compared to Taobungkhok. In Tejpur, agricultural wage along with agricultural self-employment act as a major source of livelihood in the agricultural labour households. It is well reflected in our findings that the level of occupational diversification is greatly influenced by the geographical location of the villages.

It is also reflected in our analysis that women play a distinctive role in rural economic activities in earning a livelihood for the family in both the village. It is evident from this study that on-farm employment availability for female members of agricultural labour households is much higher than the male members. In Tejpur too, days of agricultural self-employment of female members of agricultural labour households are much higher than the male members. This shows that female members of agricultural labour households play a significant role in the financial pool in the villages. On the whole, our findings show that agricultural labourers in the studied villages relied on multiple occupations, as the employment potential in each occupation is limited and seasonal. Thus, the labour markets in the studied villages do not have the structures of labour processes that are evident in the differentiated agrarian scene in rural India. The inter-locking of land, labour and credit markets affecting the labour markets are almost entirely absent in the marginal holdings based agrarian villages.

Notes: The surveys referred to in the article are parts of my doctoral thesis submitted to Manipur University.

REFERENCES

Aziz, Abdul. 1984. *Labour Problems of a Developing Economy.* New Delhi: Ashish Publishing House.

Chattopadhyay, Manbendu. 1982. Female labour in Indian agriculture. *Social Scientist* 10, 7.

Jha, Praveen. 1997. *Agricultural Labour in India.* New Delhi: Vikas Publishing House.

Kumar, B.L. 1996. Changes in the Composition of Rural Labour Force. *The Indian Journal of Labour Economics* 39, 4.

Singh, Balwinder. 2006. Decline in agricultural employment and adjustment through labour commuting: A case study from Punjab. *The Indian Journal of Labour Economics*, 49, 4.

Singh, Ng. Ibotombi. 2010. Problems and prospects of rural economy of Manipur. In *Perspective on the Economy of Manipur*, ed. by E. Bijoy Kumar Singh and Damodar Nepram. New Delhi: Akansha Publishing House.

Singh, S.P. 2006. Rural non-farm employment in Uttar Pradesh: Determinants, dimensions and regional pattern. *The Indian Journal of Labour Economics*, 49.

Singh, Seema and Bipin Kumar. 1993. Agriculture and Labour Institution in Bihar. *The Indian Journal of Labour Economics*, 36.

Vaidyanathan. A. 1986. Labour use in India: A Study of Spatial and Temporal Variations. *Economics and Political Weekly*. December.

Venkateshwaran, Sandhya. 1995. *Environment, Development and Gender Gap.* New Delhi: Sage Publcation.

White, Barbara Harris. 2004. *India Working: Essays on Society and Economy.* New Delhi: Cambridge University Press Foundation. Employment Structure of Agricultural Labourers in Manipur.

8

Anchoring India's Look East Policy

Kangujam Sanatomba

India's Look East Policy is a policy of the Government of India which seeks to forge closer economic ties with the ASEAN and other Asian tigers. The policy was initiated during the early 1990s as a response to emerging free trade regime exacerbated by globalisation. It is a part of the Structural Adjustment Programme adopted by India under pressure from international financial institutions. The Look East Policy signalled the opening up of the Indian economy to foreign capital. India's "Look East Policy" with a continental orientation, is a significant paradigm shift in its Foreign Policy.

India and South-East Asia: The Paradox

India shares close cultural ties with South-East Asia. Buddhism, which originated from India, found its followers in the East and South-East Asia on a wide scale. It was "Ashoka, The Great" who spread Buddhism far and wide in the countries of Asia. India is the cradle of this great religion and a site of pilgrimage for all the Buddhists around the world particularly the East Asian countries. It has been noted that the trees grown from cuttings of the fig tree which surrounded the eventful attainment of Enlightenment by Buddha have become objects of worship throughout the Buddhist world, and Bodh Gaya itself harbours temples financed by Thai, South Korean, and Japanese Buddhists (Jaffrelot 2003: 35-68). It is noteworthy that Buddhism is not the only point of reference that establishes deep-rooted cultural ties between India and South-East Asia.

The diverse ethnic groups of North-East India have close ethno-cultural relations with those peoples inhabiting the South-East Asian region. Similarities amongst the different peoples in the region have been the focal point of many studies. Mention has been made of the Tai-Ahoms being an offshoot of the Tai people who are called Shan in Myanmar, Thai in Thailand, Lao in Laos, Dai and Zhuang in China and Tay-Thai in Vietnam. The Meiteis of Manipur also belong to the Tai group. Racially, Nagas too belong to the Tibeto-Indonesian stock of Mongoloid family who are scattered in the north-eastern region of India and the north-western part of Myanmar. Besides many other tribes of the North-East have their ethnic kinship in South-East Asia. It has been observed that akin to the southern boundary of China that does not mark a cultural or linguistic division, India's eastern border also does not mark off a cultural or linguistic area. Emphatically speaking there are no 'natural' geographical boundaries separating South and South-East Asia along the Indo-Myanmarese border. North-East India's ties with South-East Asia in terms of historical, cultural, social and economic do not stop at these international boundaries. But, in spite of all the ethnic, linguistic and cultural affinities between India and South-East Asia, any sort of interaction, political or economic, remained very low. This could be attributed to various factors.

The colonization of South and South-East Asia by foreign powers had created an artificial spacio-temporal barrier between India and the East. History bears testimony to the fact that the Japanese occupation of Myanmar across North-East India is a critical episode which eventually led to the Indo-Myanmarese border becoming the dividing line between South and South-East Asia. The Western powers subsequently placed Myanmar within the geographical ambit of the South-East Asian Command [SEAC] during the Second World War. Even after the lapse of British paramountcy, the colonial legacy of geo-political division still lingered hampering the free interaction of people across the international boundaries. It may also be worthwhile to state that the decolonization of India, which culminated in the 'partition', rendered the north-eastern part of India a landlocked region. The geo-strategic development in the post-War period had, to a great extent, been responsible for cutting off India from the rest of Asia (Sanjib Baruah, 2004).[2]

Emergence of Cold War shattered Nehru's "Pan-Asian" dream and at the same time obstructed the opening of the "Eastern Gate" to carry on trade relations with the South-East Asian countries. The clash of ideologies and superpower activities kept the geographically contiguous regions on opposite sides of the Cold War divide. A glaring truth is that India and South-East Asian interactions remained low as a result of India's geo-political containment in South Asia by China and Pakistan. In fact, under Nehru's leadership, India tried to project itself as the leader of Asia on the basis of shared cultural affinities while attempting to keep Asia away from the US and Soviet-led blocs through the doctrine of Non-alignment. After decolonization, the campaign for pan-Asian solidarity lost much of its previous relevance. Besides, the South-East Asian countries showed more inclination towards China. It was demonstrated in the Bandung Conference of 1955 where the East Asian delegates rallied around China's leadership. Consequently, India was severely humiliated and isolated. Chinese influence in this South-East Asia prevented the countries of the region—with the exception of Malaysia—from supporting India during the 1962 Sino-Indian War (Jaffrelot 2003, 35-68).

The development of Western led alliance, the growing ties between China and Pakistan and the Indo-Soviet alliance effectively served to cut it off from South-East Asia for decades. India, on her part, also viewed the Association of South-East Asian Nations (ASEAN) with suspicion and perceived it as a disguised instrument of the West. Thus, India remained isolated from South-East Asian nations except Vietnam from mid 1950s to 1980s.

India's LEP: A Child of Economic Reforms

India's Look East Policy is a logical extension of its policy of economic liberalization, which was introduced in the year 1991 with the then Finance Minister Manmohan Singh (now the Prime Minister) as the chief architect. When Narasimha Rao came to power in 1991, a foreign exchange crisis of major proportions, besides a decline in industrial production, had overtaken India. The country faced acute crisis particularly in the Balance of Payments (BoP) position with foreign exchange reserves for only one week of its needs. An urgent and acutely felt need was immediate access to substantial amounts of foreign exchange to tide over the crisis, and this assistance was available on less than forbidding terms only from the international financial institutions like the World Bank and the Asian Development Bank, with their large American and Japanese presence respectively. Earlier India had relied upon Soviet economic and political support. Disintegration of the Soviet Union was a crucial factor in compelling the Indian Government to embark upon a programme of free market restructuring at home as it began to seek new markets and economic partners abroad. Such a shift in its economic policy was designed to attract foreign investments. In the process, its foreign policy also underwent drastic changes and more so in its perception towards South-East Asia. India had been under pressure from the Bretton Woods institutions to reform its economic structure so as to ensure the incoming of foreign capital.

India's LEP can, thus, be viewed as a response to its weak economy. It has been launched as a policy alternative in the aftermath of 'economic liberalization' which gave greater focus to economic issues and concerns (Pradhan 2005, 33-35). India's policy of Look East is a direct ramification of globalization in so far as it implies interconnectedness of the countries in the form of trade activities, flow of financial and human capital, transfer of technologies, etc. India's Look East Policy can be assessed from three main dimensions—Political, Economic and Strategic.

Political Dimension

Karl Marx wrote in the *New York Times* that the Pacific Ocean would become the Ocean of the future around which human life would concentrate, like the Mediterranean in the ancient times and the Atlantic during the Industrial Revolution (Chandra 1994, 339). Gorbachev also stated that the Asia Pacific region is currently the place where civilization is stepping up its pace (Chandra 1994, 340). The growing importance of the Asia-Pacific region led analysts and commentators remark that the world's entering the Pacific's century. Anticipation holds the region as the focus of world politics in the twentyfirst century. With the emerging situations in the Asia-Pacific region, the importance of South-East Asia has increased manifold. Its geo-political and strategic implications play a significant role in the maintenance of Balance of Power in Asia.

The political developments around the globe in the early 1990s necessitated a change in India's foreign policy. With the disappearance of the Soviet Union from the international political scenario India had lost one of its most reliable and time-tested ally. India was literally left with no reliable friend. So it became imperative for India to look for an alternative alliance and "Look East" was the product of the search for an alternative. Some opined that it was started as a long-term policy alternative in the Congress regime and after former Prime Minister Narasimha Rao's visits to the East in the early 1990s, a policy continued thereafter. Another former Prime Minister I.K. Gujral saw it as a process of redefining neighbourhood (Pradhan 2005, 33-35).

With the virtual end of the Cold War and the disintegration of erstwhile Soviet Union, bipolar international system was replaced by a 'New World Order'. In such a changed international situation, the relevance of the Non-Aligned Movement (NAM) was undermined to a great extent. The Non-Aligned Movement had been emasculated by the collapse of leadership, with a leading country like Yugoslavia embroiled in its own identity crisis. The Gulf War had greatly weakened the movement and the demise of the USSR accentuated the crisis. Robert Mugabe, the President of Zimbabwe doubted the continuing validity of the movement in the new international situation. The Prime Minister Mahathir Mohammad of Malaysia even went to the extent of rechristening the NAM and reformulating its principles and objectives. Earlier, NAM was used by India as an alternative to bloc politics to promote and protect its national interests. However, decreasing popularity of the NAM and its relevance in the changing international scenario compelled India to opt for a new political alliance with the South-East Asian countries that crystallized in the evolution of the Look East Policy as an alternative to NAM.

The collapse of the Soviet Union also created a sort of 'power vacuum' in the Asia-Pacific region. As China made swift attempts to fill in this vacuum, India could not remain a silent spectator. India wants to check the expanding influence of China in South-East Asia and East Asia. It is clear that India faces stiff competition from China for influence in South-East Asia. India looks forward to American support as the United States also seeks to impede China's increasing links with ASEAN (Kumara 2005). As such, India's Look East Policy also evolved partly as a strategy to contain China. Analyst had observed that New Delhi's current interest is in building strong, pragmatic partnerships born out of growing economic interdependence and a possible Indian role in a US led containment of China. At the moment, there is convergence of interests between India and the U.S. in so far as the containment of China is concerned.

India's Look East Policy can also be seen as a politics of engagement with the South-East Asian countries with an aim to secure a foothold in South China Sea in order to facilitate further access to the Far East. The future of India's strategic and economic interests lies in the Asia-Pacific region. Therefore, India has to pursue Pan-Asianism under the new garb called Look East Policy. It is intended to intensify diplomatic relations with South-East Asia while keeping the West aloof. India wants to evolve a new regional arrangement where it can exercise a leading role thereby increasing its bargaining power *vis-à-vis* the West.

Economic Dimension

India's Look East Policy is an external component of India's economic reforms initiated in 1991. As stated earlier, India came under strong pressure from the international financial institutions and the Western countries to go for economic liberalization as a precondition for capital investment. India had to make certain compromises with its traditional path of economic development in favour of a more overt capitalist model. Being confronted with acute financial crisis India did not have any option but to succumb to the dictates of the global capital. Thus, in this sense, India's economic liberalization is a response to globalization and LEP is a part of India's economic adjustment to the changing international economic order.

India's engagement with ASEAN as part of the Look East policy began with Sectoral Dialogue Partnership in 1992 that was upgraded to a full dialogue partnership in 1995 and a membership of the ASEAN Regional Forum in 1996. Apart from this, new initiatives for regional groupings like Mekong-Ganga Co-operation and the BIMST-EC emerged. Pankaj Jha observes that BIMST-EC is an important element in India's "Look East" strategy and adds a new dimension to India's economic co-operation with South-East Asian countries (Jha 2005, 49-51). In fact, such a trend towards regional integration is part of the larger process of globalization as Dr. Manmohan Singh stated in the first BIMST-EC Summit held at Bangkok that regional integration is not antithetical to globalization, but can be a useful building bloc. In order to survive and catch up with the pace of globalization, the engagement with the ASEAN became inevitable. In this regard, an Indian business professional said that if India wants to truly get into the globalization bus, it should first try and get into the shuttle of ASEAN. Through ASEAN, India wants to get access to the Asia-Pacific region for promoting India's strategic and economic interests. This can be seen in the official declaration made by Prime Minister Narasimha Rao in 1994 during his visit to Singapore. He categorically mentioned that the Asia-Pacific could be the springboard for our leap into the global market place (Jaffrelot 2003, 35-68). From this it becomes quite obvious that the opening of the 'Eastern Gate' has been meticulously executed with a far-sighted vision of integrating the Indian economy with the international market through association with the South-East Asian countries.

Certain positions have maintained that economy has been the prime mover of India's Look East Policy. The Look East Policy of India has been formulated because of its own weak economy and the rise of Chinese economic power. In fact, China has overtaken the US in spreading its influence in the ASEAN in political, economic and strategic terms. ASEAN perception has begun to view China less of a threat and more of a partner. In the Asian financial crisis of 1997 China refused to devalue its currency in order to help stabilize the Asian currency market. Such a benevolent attitude of China has increased its leverage in the ASEAN. Many have noted the immense potential of China-ASEAN free trade agreement. If it materializes, it would change the face of Asia and it would be the largest free trade market in the world of about 1.7 billion people. It is a mighty prospect India cannot ignore. (ICWA Foreign Affairs Report 2003, 34-40) Such kinds of economic competition from China also compelled India to pursue its Look East Policy.

Another factor that shaped India's LEP is the failure of SAARC as a regional economic bloc. SAARC has been greatly incapacitated due to the persisting conflict between India and Pakistan. It is a fact that Pakistan always tried to use the SAARC forum to discuss bilateral issues in spite of India's strong opposition to such moves. Chronic internal political disputes and wrangling have stalled any meaningful dialogue between the member-countries for evolving prospective regional co-operation and economic integration. Such a failure induced India to find an alternative regional forum and the ASEAN becomes the only option for India. In fact, since the time when India's Look East Policy was first conceived, the total trade between India and ASEAN countries has doubled. It emerged as the third largest foreign investor in India after the US and the EU. Presently ASEAN has as much to offer, perhaps, more to India than India has to offer to ASEAN. Hence, the relationship is seen mutually beneficial in largely economic terms (Sheereen 2005, 7-15). The results of India's effort to attract East and South-East Asian capital and to develop financial links have not been negligible.

In the last few years, India has started to pursue its 'Look East Policy' more vigorously than ever before. The changing global dynamics contributed significantly to this move. The stand-off between the developing countries particularly India and the advanced western countries at the W.T.O. as demonstrated in the Doha Round (2001) and the Cancun Meeting (2003) led India to search for an alternative avenue for carrying out smooth trade. Moreover, engagement with the ASEAN and other East Asian countries would give India greater leverage and bargaining power *vis-à-vis* the developed countries. Unless the Asian countries unite, they will not be able to deal with USA's unilateral economic measures. They also expressed dissatisfaction with the solutions offered by the IMF and other Western countries to their economic problems.

South-East Asia is a region with high economic potential. It has a number of export items like rice, tin, rubber, petroleum, etc. The region is also rich in vegetation and minerals. The area covering Burma, Thailand and Vietnam is known as the 'rice bowl' of Asia. Today, the Asia-Pacific region has emerged as the fastest growing region. It is believed that the focus of international trade will shift from the Atlantic to the Pacific. The region has emerged as the largest repository of raw materials, manpower, market and manufacturing.

The region accounts for 40 per cent of global trade and is the market of about 3,000 million people and 60 per cent of world's gross national product. Thus, the abundant natural resources and the future prospect of international trade in this region greatly shaped India's Look East Policy.

Another economic factor accounting for India's Look East Policy is the need for alternative energy sources. The Iraqi invasion of Kuwait and subsequent Gulf War immensely affected India in terms of petroleum imports. After the 1991 War in the Persian Gulf, the European Union and particularly the United States began to exercise monopoly over the production and sale of petroleum. India's energy policy could no longer rely upon the Middle East and this changing international situation warranted a radical shift in India's oil diplomacy. In this regard, it may be noted that the South-East Asian region has huge petroleum reserve. So, it is hoped that South-East Asia could provide India with energy necessary for its industrial expansion. The most potential sources of oil and gas are Burma and Indonesia. In January 2005, India signed an agreement in principle with Burma and Bangladesh to build a pipeline from Burmese offshore gas fields *via* Bangladesh to India (Kumara 2005). It is pertinent to note that concerns for energy sources also constitute a key factor in shaping India's Look East Policy.

Security and Strategic Dimension

India's Look East Policy is guided more by defence and strategic interests and less by economic compulsion. India's desire to extend its influence in a region where China is rapidly increasing its influence and the prospect of access to North-East for tourism and international markets can be perceived as strategic factors in the formulation of India's Look East Policy. The partition of India and the Cold War had serious implications in India's relations with its neighbours. Indeed, India wanted to redefine its relations with hostile neighbours due to increasing security concerns. The policy may thus be seen on account of India's desperate need to have friendly neighbours (Bhagat Oinam 2005).

The rise of China as a military power in Asia and its expanding influence in the Asia-Pacific region, more particularly in South-East

Asia is a matter of great concern for India. Therefore, developing strategic ties with the South-East Asian countries to counter Chinese dominance in the region has become a national priority and a capstone of India's Look East Policy. China's help to the Myanmar government with telecommunication network in Northern Myanmar is seen by India with suspicion (Bhagat Oinam 2005). There is also a Chinese plan to construct a 1,350 km railway track through Laos, Myanmar and China going up to Thailand. Both the countries have also exchanged high level visits. Ever increasing Chinese presence all along the Myanmar border is perceived as a direct threat to India's security.

Both China and India have ambitions to play more important roles in the region rendering Myanmar an area of contention between the two powers. For China, Myanmar is an important component of its strategy to prevent its encirclement by the US and its allies and to secure vital naval routes to oil supplies from the Middle East. For New Delhi, Chinese influence in Myanmar is a threat to India's plans for naval dominance in the Bay of Bengal and an obstacle to its grander aspirations for economic and strategic influence in South-East Asia (Kumara 2005). China can monitor Indian naval movements in the eastern Indian Ocean from Beijing's Signal Intelligent (SIGINT) site on Myanmar's Great Coco Island. In order to check Chinese strategic incursions into the Indian Ocean, India is backing Vietnam and Indonesia to counter Chinese dominance in the region. India is also planning to evolve a long term security alliance with the South-East Asian nations. To this end, India has initiated a number of high-level political and military visits with Vietnam, Indonesia, Singapore, Cambodia, Thailand and Myanmar as part of India's Look East Policy. India has entered the ASEAN Regional Forum (ARF), a sort of military co-operation among the ASEAN Nations which was given shape in 1994. In March 2000, the Indian Defence Minister visited Hanoi and signed a wide-ranging bilateral agreement with Vietnam paving way for mutual military co-operation. On January 11, 2001 during the Indian Prime Minister's visit to Indonesia, five agreements were signed including the landmark 'Agreement on Co-operative Activities' in the field of defence. Such diplomatic manoeuvres were aimed at normalizing relations with Vietnam. It may be recalled that Indonesia had openly supported Pakistan during the 1965 Indo-Pak war and even raised territorial claims over the Andaman and Nicobar Islands, which naturally affected India's interests in the region.

The South-East Asian countries were actually apprehensive about the expansion of Indian naval power and possible growing influence of India in the region. It is important to note that India's regional engagement with the South-East Asian countries has been undertaken to ensure military security for the Andaman and Nicobar Islands in addition to the safeguarding of India's maritime interests in the Indian Ocean. In its maritime doctrine released in April 2004, the Indian Navy shifted its doctrine from defending the country's coastline from rival Pakistan to monitoring the entire Indian Ocean region (IOR), from the Persian Gulf to the Malacca Straits which it perceives to be its legitimate area of interest (IBID). It may be stated that while the Andaman and Nicobar Islands are 800 miles away from the Indian Coast, it is only 20 miles from Myanmar, 90 miles from Indonesia and 250 miles from Thailand and Malaysia.

On the other hand, the United States' recent engagement with Bangladesh showing a possible shift in its military base from Pakistan in a possible deterioration of Afghanistan crisis is equally concerning for India. Parallel with this, the ISI of Pakistan use Bangladesh as a safe haven from where they could operate with ease. There is also every possibility that any terrorist operation including activities such as piracy, arms-smuggling and drugs, etc., in South-East Asia has the potential of spilling over to the Andaman and Nicobar Islands. Maj. Gen. Afsar Karim said that different terrorist groups like Jamaah Islamia, Jaish-e-Mohammad, etc., operating in various countries, had now come under one roof, *i.e.*, Al-Qaeda. He said that after 9/11, Al-Qaeda had shifted its main base to Pakistan and began operating in various places like Central Asia, South Asia with the help of local terrorist outfits (ICWA Foreign Affairs Reports 2003, 34-41). Such security concerns also serve as motivating factors of India's Look East Policy.

Keeping these security compulsions in view, India had signed two broad agreements, for comprehensive economic co-operation and combating terrorism with the ASEAN. Speaking on the subject in an address to the Institute of Diplomatic and Foreign Relations in Kuala Lumpur on May 16, 2001, Vajpayee had articulated his vision of a new South-East Asian security structure and India's role in it. Vajpayee had said that security problems had to be tackled through a co-operative approach, holistically and regionally, as there could be no effective solution to those problems within the national boundaries. He stated that threats like religious extremism, drug trafficking, money laundering and terrorism had cast a dark shadow over South and South-East Asia and deplored that India has been a victim of state-sponsored and cross-border terrorism seeking to redraw national boundaries. He emphasized that security dialogue between India and ASEAN is of utmost importance (Shehin, 2003).

On November 5, 2003, the then External Affairs Minister, Yashwant Sinha said that India's Look East policy had entered phase-II, which is more comprehensive in its coverage, territorially and politically. Expressing his views on strategic concerns of India's Look East Policy he spoke of a consensus within India that this is a goal of prosperity which should be pursued with single-minded determination. He calls it the reason behind India's desire for peace and cooperation with all the forces fighting terrorism (*The Hindu* Online Edition, Thursday, November 06, 2003). In his view, the forces which have taken to terrorism will be subdued soon because the fight against terrorism is becoming global. From these it seems quite evident that combating terrorism also constitutes an essential ingredient of India's Look East Policy.

More covertly, India's interest is guided by internal security. The existence of various armed insurgent groups in the North-Eastern part of India having base camps in Myanmar and Bangladesh is a matter of serious security concern. The presence of North-East insurgents across the international borders has caused a lot of security anxieties for India. Therefore, India wants both Burma and Bangladesh to act against these insurgents operating on their soils.

In recent years, the Burmese government launched a military crackdown on various armed insurgent groups of India taking shelter in the country. The Burmese military also sealed its border to block the insurgents when the Indian military forces launched a major operation code-named "Operation All Clear" involving 6,000 troops to crack down the rebels in Manipur during 2004-05. But the extent to which the Burmese authority would co-operate with India in dealing with the insurgents remains uncertain. General perception indicates the Burmese military's discord with the Indian army for circulating fake currency notes that seriously affected the Burmese economy. Controversy between the two countries regarding the border issue still persists. The Indian government also provides political asylum to the leaders of Burmese democratic movements while at the same time harbouring the Burmese insurgent groups on the Indian side.

In 1996 when Sheikh Hasina came to power, the Bangladesh government launched a sweeping operation against the militants of the North-East operating in the country which included freezing of all their bank accounts. But when Begum Khaleda Zia returned to power, the operations ceased. It is worth mentioning that Bangladesh has been hostile towards India since its inception in 1971 partly because of India's big brotherly attitude and fear of its economy being exploited by India. As a matter of policy Bangladesh has recently denied harbouring any camps of the North-East insurgent groups. It may also be recalled that the Indian government had provided all sorts of assistance to the rebel groups of the Chittagong Hill Tract (CHT) against the Bangladesh government. In turn, Bangladesh retaliated in the same manner.

India has keen interest in establishing security and strategic co-operation with ASEAN because of its population, geography, maritime sea-lanes and natural resources. The ASEAN is a gateway to the Asia-Pacific region where lies the focus of global security in the Twenty-first century. All these security and strategic considerations drove India to seek closer relations with South-East Asian countries.

Concluding Remarks

The United States is bent on containing China through encirclement policy. Today, the US is trying to pose India against China, a balancing role that was applied to India with Pakistan as a counter-balance during and after the cold war. Viewed in this context, India's Look East Policy will naturally fit into the US strategy of expanding its influence in the region by restricting China. Because, the strategic interests of the US and India stand complementary as far as China is concerned since India's Look East policy is covertly to compete with China. India is only trying to avoid giving such an impression on account of diplomatic expediency. Nevertheless, India has been collaborating with the US in containing China. But such a short-sighted foreign policy decision-making would prove to be counter-productive in the long run. If China decides to make counter moves, India will lose one of her neighbours at the altar of the American imperialist game plan. It is in India's interest to redefine its perception towards China and forge an Asian solidarity through structural re-alignment in order to check the US led neo-imperialism of the Western capitalist countries.

A fundamental question coming from analysts and commentators revolve round India's desire to give its Look East Policy a continental orientation. The question assumes critical proportions as India had maintained a maritime outlook *vis-à-vis* South-East Asia all along. Sanjib Baruah had stated that it is cheaper and less troublesome for India to trade with South-East Asia by sea rather than by land. In fact, the security anxiety of India due to existence of numerous insurgent outfits in the North-East has been a major factor in shaping India's LEP. In this context, Sanjib Baruah foregrounds the argument that it is India's security anxiety—getting Myanmar to act against North-East Indian insurgent groups that take shelter in Myanmar—rather than a desire to give the Look East Policy a continental orientation that explains India's U-turn *vis-à-vis* Myanmar (Sanjib Baruah 2004, 25). India wants to crush insurgency in the North-East sooner than later. Therefore, on the pretext of operationalising Look East Policy, India will have to call in more and more military forces which will have serious implications on the state of human rights in the North-East given the past records of the Indian military and para-military forces.

In spite of the claim made by many observers that economy has been the prime mover of India's Look East Policy (LEP), the government have not sufficiently built up necessary infrastructures and supportive institutional mechanisms in the border areas to facilitate the smooth implementation of the said policy. The much hyped LEP remain only on paper. Besides, diplomatic activities and exchange of visits seem heavily confined to strategic and security areas only. India is more interested in persuading both Bangladesh and Myanmar to take action against the North-East insurgent groups operating from their countries rather than preparing the ground for expediting the execution of bilateral trade. Moreover, India has been able to secure Vietnamese co-operation for imparting guerrilla training to the Indian army for counter-insurgency operation in the North-East. Therefore, as long as India remains obsessed with its internal security concerns, no tangible outcome can be expected from the much publicised Look East Policy.

On the whole, India's Look East Policy is apparently a part of the larger capitalist strategy of containing China and capturing the South-East Asian markets while simultaneously extracting raw-material from the region and exploiting the cheaper labour force. The involvement of huge metropolitan capital in the development of transnational trading infrastructure vindicates this truth. India is a loyal camp follower of the US led imperialism in South-East Asia. In this context, India needs to reorient its Look East Policy if it wants to survive the onslaught of globalization. Firstly, while pursuing the Look East Policy, India should not engage in conflict with China by collaborating with the United States. America is not a reliable ally and it may soon reverse its attitude towards India with the changing international situation. Besides, India should remember that the US is siding with Pakistan against India in the same manner it is doing with India against China. As such, India should not miss the opportunity of buiiding a close relationship with the Asian countries, which was earlier stalled due to historical circumstances. India should join hands with the Asian countries in checking the expansion of American hegemony in the region. India needs to redefine its foreign policies in line with the emerging circumstances.

REFERENCES

Baruah, Sanjib. (2004). "Between South and South-East Asia: North-East India and the Look East Policy". Guwahati: CENISEAS.

Chandra, Prakash, (1994). *International Relations*. New Delhi: Vikas Publishing House.

ICWA Foreign Affairs Report, (2003). "India-ASEAN: Evolving Strategic Partnership". *Indian Council of World Affairs*, Vol. 2, Nos. 7-12, July-December, pp. 34-40.

Jaffrelot, Christophe. (2003). "India's Look East Policy: Asianist Strategy in Perspective". In *India Review*, Vol. 2, No. 2, April: 35-68.

Jha, Pankaj. (2005). "BIMST-EC: A New Regional Initiatives". *South Asia Politics*, May: 49-51.

Kumara, Sarath. (2005). "Burma Visit Highlights India's 'Look East' Strategy",

India, 6th April 2005 <http://www.wsws.org/articles/2005/apr2005/india06_prn.shtml>

Oinam, Bhagat. (2005). "Manipur" in Mayumi Murayama *et al.* (Eds). 2005. *Sub-Regional Relations in the Eastern South Asia: With special focus on India's North-Eastern Region.* Tokyo, Japan:Yugengaisha Tohkohsha.

Pradhan, Radhe Gopal. (2005). "India's Look East Policy: A Holistic Policy". In *South Asia Politics*, May: 33-35.

Sheereen, Zeba. (2005). "Regionalism and Economic Opportunities for India-SAARC or ASEAN". *Third Concept,* April, 2005. pp. 7-15.

Sultan, Shehin, (2003). India's 'Look East' Policy Pays off, *Asia Times*, October 11, 2003, http://www.global_policy.org/globaliz/econ/2003/1011indiaasean.htm.

The Hindu, Online Edition, Thursday, Nov. 06, 2003. "Look East Policy not Restricted to ASEAN: Sinha" <http://www.hindu.com/thehindu/2003/11/06stories/2003110605151100htm.>

Part – III
Understanding Resistance

9
Mapping Repressive Practices against Women in the Meitei Society

Shreema Ningombam

2004 July 15 nude protest by women in Manipur had left an ineffaceable picture on the minds of many "outsiders" within India and beyond. The "imagined" fairy/ghostly land that existed only in a corner of the mindscape for the moment seemed to have broken free from its cocooned "self" and it emerged out of the shell crawling and roaring. The phenomenon arrested the attention of the "other/s" like never before. Many of the even the so-called "informed" observers from outside the State were awe-struck by the flaming spectacle. No other incidents in Manipur must have befuddled their imagination than the 12 nude women protesting in front of the Kangla Fort then occupied by the Indian armed forces.

The episode drew more attention than the series of violent demonstrations that preceded it. The protesting image of the *Imas* (mothers) or the *Meira Paibis* (torch-bearers) became the "signifier" of a society in, which women seems to take leading roles in all spheres of life. Any imagery of Manipur seems incomplete without some captured images of the *Imas* protesting or the "Ima market" in Imphal. These images conjure up the precious sense of women being truly powerful in our society. But do these images truly reflect the reality beneath the surface? Well chronicled social upheavals in Manipur are testimonies to how we as women have mobilised ourselves or responded to actions in the "public spheres" read as streets, "*leikai*" (community) gatherings and the numerous "*keithels*" (local markets).

The response and the participation of women in these circumscribed public sphere is not so much due to the fact that women in Manipur are more powerful, skilled or educated or provided with sufficient opportunities. Rather, the continuing lack of modern normative and institutional practices, and hierarchies of tradition have led to the emergence of such an image and role of women. In such circumstances, women are forced to take the responsibility of offsetting the fallout of the political turmoil and economic hardships (Patra and Manna 2008, 23). The lingering complexities of modernity and tradition have posed strong incongruence between the reality and projected images of the women in our society.

There are certain universal approaches to the question of women's life and rights. In addition, there are also various customs and practices that have systematically subordinated/repressed women to certain conditions, which are not as visible as the numerous protests/marches/demonstrations in the valley streets by women or as real as women selling various products at the *Ima Keithel* (mothers' market) in the heart of Imphal, the capital of Manipur. The subordination or repression is even made worse by the whirling political conflicts and subsequent militarization. This does not, however, stop us from probing into how women have been marginalised through acquired customs and practices like in any other patriarchal societies.

"Naturalness" of Women's Subjugation

There is a pervasive dominant belief that women are naturally inferior to men. It is assumed that they are not only by nature physically weaker than men but also mentally inferior. This belief is very well entrenched in our age-old social customs, practices and laws. We are so blinded and conditioned by these very understanding that we do not even dare question if these ideas of the "inferior" are natural or not. Prominent social scientists, anthropologists and sociologists around the world have contended that there is nothing natural in this world in terms of human behaviour or custom. Every minute act is socially, historically and linguistically constructed and even that the so called "instincts" are learned and taught. In other words, every social norm or act is legitimised through conventions made and enforced by men for perpetuating a power structure most suited to them under the structure of patriarchy. The initial understanding that sex is related to nature while gender is related to culture has been reworked considerably. As Judith Butler puts it, gender is not the cultural inscription of meaning on a pre-given sex rather gender as a way of thinking or a concept produces the category of biological sex (Butler 1993, 23). Even the legitimization of heterosexuality and stigmatization of homosexuality have developed through a historically charted contour.

What made these developments possible is the historical process of the *status quoists* (men) to perpetuate their power at the cost of the less powerful (women). The contention put forth here will become clearer as we go from the universal to the local specificities. Another often repeated age-old stereotype is that women are born to care and nurture children, adults and even animals and plants. The work of nurses, attendants, helpers, therapists, maids, *etc*., or any activity related to burst the stress of man or women or children in even today's supposedly modern world are the domain allotted predominantly to women.

The attribution given to the "ordained" duty of women as natural is one of the major factors that have contributed to gender subordination and repression besides stereotyping. It has become normal to believe that household duties are universal and natural duties of women. All contributions by women within the family are unproductive and unpaid, thus, consequently remain unrecognised and devalued. But the productivity of men in the public domain is made possible only because of women's occupation of the responsibilities in the private domain. This responsibility gives men the much needed time and space to pursue paid or unpaid labour in the public domain. The issue here is not a demand for payment of labour of nurturing or caring by a mother but a demand for recognition of the value and productivity of the very work done by women in the private sphere.

Meitei Society: Reinforcing Patriarchy

Patriarchy cannot be understood as discrete individual behaviour of a patriarch or the male head of the family. Rather we find in our society a system of social relations that perpetuate the exploitation of women by men. The exploitation of a person or an object is preconditioned by its control in some form or the other. Control of female sexuality and procreativity are the basis of men's control over women (Lerner 1986, 12). In Meitei society, the domination of women is executed by controlling their sexuality, access to meaningful decision making participation and by appropriating the symbols attach to women's attire and body. The moral baggage that is put upon the women's shoulders under which she is expected to abstain from pre-marital sex and confine to sex with her husband only after marriage is overtly "honoured" and termed as the "prestige" of the society as a whole, which is just one of the many ways of controlling the female sexuality. On the contrary, a man's exhibition of his sexual prowess and gratification is legitimised through cultural and social legitimization of polygamy despite the contemporary legal disdain to such practices. Thus, man in patriarchal system is exempted from carrying the burden of "idealised" sexual morality.

Although patriarchy existed in our society from its pre-modern era, it is with the development of complex agricultural (semi-feudal) economy and the advent of Hinduism and the ongoing political turmoil in the State that it has taken such stringent form and content. As the society became more complex in terms of means and relations of production, the division of labour, too, became more differentiated resulting in a more hierarchised social structure. The valley developed a more complex agricultural economy comparing to the surrounding highlands. Certain traits of semi-feudalism had existed in our society. Perhaps, this fact coupled with new Brahmanical ethos that relegated women to the domestic sphere gave an impetus to the entrenchment of patriarchal system in Meitei society.

Advent of Hinduism and Crystallization of Patriarchy

The advent of Hinduism and the mode of its arrival in our society could be another factor that had exacerbated the already existing patriarchal system. Unlike the initial phase of Bhakti or the *Gaudiya Vaishnava* movement elsewhere in India, the strand that reached Manipur was not grown out of a social movement as understood in its historical sense. The Bhakti movement began from the grassroots led by figures mainly drawn from the lower strata of the society. The basic tenet of the *Bhakti* movement was the elimination of the concept of the "intermediary" between a devotee and God. The movement emphasised that just by chanting the Lord's name, anyone from the lowest or the highest caste can reach him directly. Brahminical order, which was characterised by a highly inequitable social order, was the precondition for the rise of the *Bhakti* movements in the rest of India. Hinduism and its variants reached Manipur *via* the political route and it was imposed on its people by subsequent royal decrees assisted by migrant Brahmins. This was followed by a process of proselytization and a resultant fusion of Meitei worldview and Hindu worldview.

When Vaishnavism reached Manipur it also brought along with it certain practices, which went against the prevailing gender equations hardly known to this land earlier. The construction of an ideal woman in terms of Hindu world view, association of women with pollution and purity, certain practice of ostracism of women, exclusion of women in rituals, the division between those embracing Hinduism and those who refused to accept the new faith, banning of eating meat, consumption of liquor, the practice of burial substituted by cremation are some practices that had seeped into the social polity of Manipur after the advent of Hinduism in Manipur. It is interesting to note that the sites of pilgrimage such as *Varuni Ching* (Varuni Hill), *Koubru Lekha* (a site of pilgrimage) and the temple at Mahabali became the symbols of the new faith that have gradually been internalised in the minds of the Meiteis. This process was actively assisted by those who could appropriate the most in the new social order constructed with sanctions from the palace.

Nature of Political Decay

One of the main reasons that have perpetuated deep-rooted patriarchal practices in the current context is the nature of crises of governability in Manipur over the years. The pace of institutional development is lagging much behind the level of expectations, demands and needs of the people. This is further compounded by political conflicts and armed violence. The complete dysfunctional state of governance and the resultant scarcity of resources makes the people feel helpless and insecure. The situation has led to the subsequent erosion of mutual trust and desire of a collectivity among the people. Over the years, common men have been seeking security in a crisis-ridden economy and in turn women have been seeking security by marrying financially and materially sound men. A woman is forced to take recourse to the patriarchal and conventional definition of what is "attractiveness", "beauty" and "chastity", which enable her to enhance her unique selling points (USP) in the marriage market.

Though, highly enviable, her education and the potential to become an economically independent "being" remain secondary. The rise of "exhibitionism" of *Awunpot* (dowry) in our society in the last few decades speaks for itself. The conflictual nature of our polity has further lowered the already subordinate position of women. The structure of political violence and State repression adds other layers of complexities to the gender equation in Manipur. Hence, we have a situation where women are now advised not to venture out in public space after dark for fear of being raped or molested by the armed forces or armed thugs. No wonder, women are gradually made to withdraw from taking a full-fledged participation in public affairs in terms of political negotiations and decision making process.

Repression of Women: Symbols and Possible Meanings

Subordination and oppression of women in Meitei society can be analysed from various practices both symbolic and real. Beginning with the caution that the practices I shall be analyzing are not the outcome of generalization rather, they are random selections from my discussions with colleagues and my own observations. The first thing I would like to take up is the issue of touching man's feet by his wife at least on the day of elopement or on the day of marriage. The English term elopement is used usually with a negative connotation as it is an act of running away of the lovers against the wish of her parents or societal norms. But in the Meitei society the act of elopement has a positive connotation. It is positive in the sense that more often than not the act is performed at times with full consent of her parents in order to legitimise a forthcoming or a pending marriage. It has a social acceptance in the Meitei society. Secondly, married women in some households eat only after their husbands and in-laws have eaten. Thirdly, in any religious feasts or *Ushob* the highest pedestal is occupied by the patriarchs and women are further excluded in any serious ritual practices. Fourthly, the ostracization of women during their menstrual cycle termed as *mangba* or "being impure" shall be discussed. Next, I would like to take up the issue of serving the wife with the leftover of her husband's on the day of marriage. Again there are the predefined essential social qualities for a *yatra-pubi/lai pubis* or ritual parade leader and the stigma attached to a woman who had eloped but not married and last but not the least, the issue of the notion of the sight of *phanek*, a kind of sarong/wraparound worn by Meitei women, as inauspicious.

Subservient Touch and the World of Leftovers

In the existing plethora of art, literature or folklore of the land, there is nothing to suggest instances of women touching her husband's feet predating the coming of Hinduism in Manipur. This suggests that there is ample evidence that this practice proliferated after most Meiteis became Vaishnav Hindus. One should clearly understand the subtle difference between *Luk Nonba* and the "touching of the feet". The virtual motive behind this act is to show a mark of respect or reverence or love to their husbands. The real motive ingrained deeply in the act is that women are subservient or subordinated to their men folk. If this symbolic act is just to represent respect or reverence, why do men refrain from doing the same to their wives? Obviously, they do the same to their mother. The underlying text or the sub-text behind this act seems to suggest that women lay at the mercy of their husbands and their egos. A woman with all her sense of objectivity and subjectivity will constantly question the existing *status quo*. Nevertheless, it is left to the moral responsibility of those who choose to opt for an equitable society regardless of sex or gender, so that they can at least rationalise the act or denounce it as an act of domination and oppression.

The phenomenon of women eating only after their husbands and male family members have eaten might have lost its relevance to most of my readers who hail from open and nuclear families. But this act is still in practice in some of the families. The very phenomenon denies the women the right to eat whenever they are hungry. One might argue that women perform such acts with their own consent but one fails to realise that this very act is constructed and ingrained in the minds of women through the process of socialization "to be feminine". In the first formal dinner as a member of her husband's family, the wife in the nuptial night is served with the leftover, *chak aremba,* of her husband. Mostly, the custom is executed nominally without even knowing the meaning and the purpose of the performance. The problem here is the meaning, the hidden intention and the latent idea that the act carries and symbolises. The act symbolises the wife's subordinate position to her husband from the first conjugal night onwards. It symbolises man's domination over women not physically but psychologically as well. The act is considered so natural that the performer as well as those who socialises her to perform this act find nothing wrong in the custom. The norm is so entrenched that questioning it would seem like questioning the process and purpose of breathing itself.

Ostracism: Blood, Sweat and *Phanek*

During menstruation period women are not allowed to touch any "clean" object of the kitchen, they are not permitted to worship the household deities nor are they allowed to have conjugal relation at least superficially. These practices when glanced from a perspective, looks as if women have been given a weeklong vacation from the household chores, services rendered to the gods and, of course, sexual obligations to their husbands. In reality, during this period most women are made to do all the manual activities of the household ranging from wiping of floor to washing of clothes to cleaning of dishes.

There have been many who have argued that ostracization of a woman during her menstrual cycle have certain logic. If menstrual blood is considered unhygienic and unclean, it is true even for all excreted matter like urine, faeces, or sweat. There were times, when women during menstrual period were prohibited from even going near the sources of water like *leikais* (community) ponds and wells. And the state of menstruation of women during this period is called *mangba* meaning the state of being impure connoting and suggesting that women during this period are "impure". The notion of impurity of menstrual blood is a social construct to marginalise women. In some Meitei customs, piece of mother's *phanek* used at the time of birth is put inside a tiny copper cylindrical container and carried as a talisman by the woman's offspring whenever the person goes to far flung places. This was used to ward off evil spirit and ill omen. An interpretation is that the *lai-tin* (evil spirits) does not like to touch a person who is "polluted" as the person associated with her mother's piece of *phanek*, which is polluted, so, she is free from the fear of harm done by evil spirits. We can see the idea of pollution has even infiltrated the interpretation itself in later stages.

Ominous Sights, Signs and Stigmas

A Meitei man who is supposed to be "manly", *Nupa thokpa*, is to never touch a woman's *phanek* in the public. The sight of or contact with a *phanek* is considered inauspicious only when it is detached from the wearer that is when the *phanek* is lying unattended. The notion behind the custom is the understanding that *phanek* is polluted as it is or might be stained with menstrual blood or vaginal discharge, which are considered impure. The arrival of undergarments and means of remaining tidy during normal or "those" five days is a recent one as a part of certain level of modernization seeping in our State. It would be too naïve to imagine that our grandmothers and generations preceding them would have got access to such means. Even today, there are a number of women who are below poverty line and cannot get access to such means. The *phanek* as any other garments like *Khudei* (a traditional Meitei dress worn by men) or *khonggrauw* (trousers) becomes soiled after use. The custom is a very sensible one if seen from the point of view of public hygiene. The only problem here is the attachment of pollution and a sense of inauspiciousness to the sight or touch of a *phanek* regardless of its state of cleanliness or being dirty.

The custom is so entrenched that at times, the man has to helplessly watch his wife's *phanek* being drenched in the rain when the wife goes away leaving the *phanek* to dry on the clothes-line or the *polangkhok*. The customs that I have just described renders a man weak, helpless and powerless to help women related to him in spite of his desire to do so and thereby going against his will and wish because he himself is bound by the structure of patriarchy. The case of the *Yatra Pubis/Lai Pubis, Yatra Pubi*, the leading lady of the ceremony especially in marriage and *lai-haraoba* (a festival of pleasing the village deities) the ideal lady who should be leading a marriage procession should never be a woman who is a widow, whose child/children have died, who cannot bear children, who is married within her own clan (*yek-thoknaba*). In the case of *lai-haraoba*, which is a pre-Hindu festival of the local deities, the maiden who carries the objects used in worship is supposed to be a virgin. And a woman who had eloped with a man *(chellurabi nupi)*, in most cases, is not given the privilege. The foundation beneath the construction of these practices is the understanding that participation by such defiled female members in any ritual is inauspicious as our society attaches certain stigma to such woman.

The Second Sex: Defined and Defiled

Based on the above observation, a woman's health and status is defined by the health of her husband, her sons and ultimately by the health of her family. These customs exemplify how the association of a woman with a male is inevitable for the alleviation of her social status. A woman's loneliness, her inability to bear a male child or the death of her child or even the untimely death of her husband, events as such, which are completely beyond her control, are intolerable to the society and this becomes a main reason for her exclusion in rituals and celebrations. There are various other phenomena besides the ones described above on ways of defining the status and purity of a woman by associating/disassociating with a male. The society simply has no yardsticks to measure the role of men in this process of defining the second sex. What is a cause for concern is when women themselves are repeatedly made to believe in these ways of life, they themselves become instruments of perpetuating such tradition.

The need is to bring in a different perspective and vision in understanding women not only as the bearer of morality but also as human beings, as complete entities in themselves. The need is to transfer the duty of defining oneself to the object of definition herself as this object of definition is a thinking, breathing, living subject. Women are rendered powerless in all the dimensions: decision-making process, agenda setting process and even at the level of thought formation (Lukes 2005). In the family the decision making process is mostly the arena of man who is the head of the family. Our society condemns the family in, which women's say sway the decision as "effeminate" (*nupina paanba emung*). Men decide what matters are to be discussed and what matters to be left out. And to further render women powerless, the women are taught, socialised, trained and indoctrinated to be an "ideal woman". These processes are executed diligently because the cost of deviation from producing this ideal one is too much for any family to afford.

Recovery and Redefinition: Acts of Marching Forward

The peculiarity of the problem in our society needs to be understood. Basic human rights have been denied to all the people of the State for over three decades by the repressive laws of the Centre imposed upon the State. Nevertheless, we cannot wait for the resolution of the conflict and restoration of normalcy and stability as a precondition for the rectification of the gender bias. Women's problem needs to be recognised without any procrastination and the solution for political conflict cannot be holistic without the solution of gender conflict. These two problems need to be interlinked and comprehended wholly. The nationalistic question cannot be addressed independent of the questions of gender. The utmost important social change in terms of emancipation of women is a movement towards their well-being and bestowing of rights to them. The rights, however, much well bestowed cannot empower the women unless she becomes an "agent" rather than a passive recipient of rights and policies (Sen 1999, 192). Making women economically independent thereby making them free from dependence on others is a main instrument in empowering women. Women's ability to earn an independent income enhances her social standing in the household and in the society, commands respect from others and provides an opportunity in the public domain. Giving women the ownership right or the right to property is instrumental in making her more powerful and actively participate in the family decision making process. The provision of education and literacy to women will make them more informed, skilled and capable to grab available opportunities. Women themselves have to take the responsibilities of correcting the inequalities within the family doing away with the archaic inegalitarian value system and conventions. In the most tangible sense, the knowledge to maintain her own sexuality, pregnancy and childbirth in the safest possible ways should be disseminated to adult women regardless of her marital status. It is the time to recognise the difference and respect the difference as it is. And of course, courageously face the future ahead.

REFERENCES

Butler, Judith. (1993). *Bodies that Matter*. London and New York: Routledge.

Lerner, Gerda. (1986). *The Creation of Patriarchy: Volume 1-Women and History*. New York and Oxford: Oxford University Press.

Lukes, Steven. (2005). (2nd edition). *Power: A Radical View*. London: MacMillan Publications.

Patra, Soumyajit and Manna, Samita. (2008). Integrative Reconciliation: Mothers in the Naga Movements. *Economic and Political Weekly*, XLIII, 10. March 8-14: 21-5.

Sen, Amartya. (1999). *Development as Freedom*. London and New York: Oxford University Press.

10
Motherhood and the Politics of Resistance

Diana Naorem

Notion of motherhood

Out of the many issues of womanhood, motherhood got its due attention in the late 1970s and the 1980s. Since then, it has emerged as a continuing topic of debate and discussion. It remains ambivalent and contested, inadequately explained and theorised, despite ample interrogations and interventions. The definition of motherhood has become a lot more interesting than ever before. According to Maithreyi Krishnaraj, the capability of reproduction is what makes women 'mothers'. Through the act of carrying a child in her womb and giving birth, a woman attains 'motherhood' (Krishnaraj 2010, 2). But if a mother is only defined as one who gives birth to children, then the notion gets too narrowed down, to being just a biological relationship. Motherhood goes much beyond this, and includes those women, who despite having missed the reproduction process, become mothers by performing the latter part, i.e., by bringing up the child, helping him or her take shape. In the meantime, various scientific advancements[1] have expanded the conventional definition of motherhood, stretching it out to include other avenues of reproduction, involving more players and stakeholders. Consequently, debates surrounding the notion of motherhood became more complex, making any response to the question—who is a mother—a contested one. Hence, any effort to understand motherhood will have to be a multifaceted task.

The concept and ideology of motherhood has been closely associated with women and is seen as a major factor which distinguishes women from men. In some theoretical strands, it is perceived as the central fact of female existence. Motherhood is entwined with notions of femininity, and women/gender identity is enforced through motherhood (cited in Arendell 2000, 1192). It also reinforces the idea of the most desirable way of being a woman, a construct around which a range of social practices revolve. In case of failure to fulfil this role, the blame goes to women who are then stigmatised, and ostracised in the extreme cases. It further questions women's acceptability in the society, "the legitimate role of wife, her marital stability, security, bonding and her role in the family and community" (Sama 2006, 8–9). All women are seen as mothers but it would be wrong to do so. One reason for the synonymous association is the fact that all mothering work is done by women only. Though all women can be seen as potential mothers in the near and far future, not every woman becomes a mother. Mothering as a separate domain monopolised by women needs to be broken down so that the role could be shared between men and women. But, since reproduction continues to be one of the major roles of women, it has continued to be basic to women's life, and its failure thereby implying a social crisis.

Motherhood entails care and nurture and also evolves a relationship between the care giver/nurturer and the receiver. The definition of mothering shares a theme: 'the social practice of nurturing and caring of dependent children' (Arendell 2000, 1192). The mother and child relationship is conceived as purely an emotional one which entrusts upon the mother, the responsibility of bringing up the child and helping him/her develop an identity, and preparing them to go out to the social space. The intimate relation of care also involves, and has evolved, what Terry Arendell calls, 'maternal' skills. The maternal work which comprises of nurturing, protection, training, etc., according to her, receives a certain kind of response from the children driven mainly by their needs. In their active dynamic interaction, the mother develops affectionate connections with the child while the child starts to lay certain claims on the mother emotionally and morally (Leonard 1996 cited in Arendell 2000, 1194). Further the relationship extends beyond the child to a series of complex socio-economic and cultural contexts that have influenced both its understanding and practice.

Ideologically and practically associated with love and care for the child, the act and power of creation and nurturing, motherhood also portrays women as the embodiment of sacrifice and nobility. All these factors taken together, make motherhood the icon of celebration and worship, best manifested in the concept of 'motherland' and the practices of worshipping female deities. But contestations arise around questions of control over one's body, choice and agency. Feminists have addressed motherhood in different ways – the extreme poles being occupied on one side, by those who see it as inhibiting or limiting women's freedom, calling all women to renounce it, and on the other, by those who see it as a source of power and agency, standing firmly for the need to make full use of it to further their influence and agency. While we are not going into the details of the debate, it is worthwhile to point out here that motherhood is, as Sara Ruddick has said, a constant conjunction between power and powerlessness (Ruddick 1980, 343). On one side, there is pain and oppression, while on the other there is efficacy and happiness that come from her capacity to bear and nurse children. It can be thus, a source of both power and oppression depending on how it is articulated and experienced.

This article will look into the 'power' aspect of motherhood. It attempts to explore how motherhood as a trope and practice becomes a rallying principle for certain political movements, and how maternal care is related with the politics of resistance. It is often claimed that motherhood provides women a very important space where they could assert their voices and organise themselves for their entry into the political. We will explore one such case where 'motherhood' has gained a degree of success in mobilising specific struggles. The women of Manipur, united under the banner of the *Meira Paibi*, encompass a wide range of activities focussing on their democratic resistances against injustices and violence. What they demonstrate in their movements can be seen as shifting of the prescribed domain of motherhood. It is through these movements that the women choose to present themselves in the public space. The question is then, how womanhood is articulated in their resistances.

These movements are also viewed as being against the State, which in itself is a patriarchal institution. It will, therefore, be interesting to explore whether there is anything feminist about the movements and whether the articulation of motherhood in public, redefine gender roles, or conversely reinforce the oppressive dichotomy of the private and public spaces? On the other hand, when motherhood comes to play an active role in the public spaces, the question it poses is, whether the 'public-ness' of motherhood has anything to offer to these women in terms of their agency and status? How do women use the principle of 'women' as 'symbol' of home, honour, and culture, and their patriarchally ascribed role of mothering, to invert their relationship with the State and also oppose it simultaneously?

The Birth of *Meira Paibis*[2]

The women's movements all over the world have been driven by various issues of social, political and economic nature. The interesting fact about the *Meira Paibis* struggle is their emphasis on their 'biological' role as mothers and their specific grounding on ideals of motherhood. Tracing the origin of these movements based on motherhood, leads us to women's movements against human rights violation in the Latin American countries, mainly Argentina, Guatemala and Chile. Later similar struggles were accounted in Sri Lanka while the more recent cases being that in Kashmir carried forward by the Association of Parents of Disappeared Persons (APDP), and in Manipur by the *Meira Paibis*. Writing on the Latin American context, Jennifer Schirmer, called this particular form of women's movement 'motherist' movement, for the women came out as mothers rather than as women. In her opinion, these mothers fought against repression by mobilising themselves in a particular kind of protest that transformed women's language of motherhood into a kind of political expression (Schirmer 1989, 4). The movement of the *Meira Paibis* can also be categorised as 'motherist', because the women in these struggles are united by the common thread of being a 'mother'.

It has always been a proud claim that, women in Manipur had so far occupied a prominent position, with their involvement in the public and political going back to a long history. The women of all generations derived their strength from various legends and myths of prominent and powerful female deities and queens. They are further motivated by the history of women's activisms at different periods, the most revered among them being the First and Second *Nupi Lan*[3] in 1904 and 1939 respectively. The women of today and their movement can be seen to have their roots in these historical accounts. Contemporary women's activism began against alcohol and drug addiction, intervened in the form of '*Nisha Bandi*' meaning 'banning of all intoxicants'. It is a spontaneous and voluntary body of women aiming at detoxifying the society. Their activities comprised of late night vigil, roaming around the streets of their respective area/locality, targeting both liquor producers and consumers.

It was in the early 1980s that women's activism took a different turn. The 80s saw major insurgent groups having strong foothold, executing numerous violent offensives against the Armed Forces. The Armed Forces, indeed armed with extraordinary powers, retaliated at full swing, worst of all without distinguishing between an insurgent, and a civilian. This is generally evident in militarist policy of the State with primary consideration for national security, which looks at any movement for self-determination as 'foreign instigated' and one that should be crushed. Consequently they gave main emphasis on dealing with 'law and order' equating the problem as one arising out of law and order failure. The perceived national threats legitimised the State's militarist responses. Militarism, as Anuradha M. Chenoy noted, became an entrenched element in State policies, prominent since the 1980s in the North-East, with policies and programmes grounded in it, rather than addressing the social, developmental and political issues (Chenoy 2002, 127-28). It was against this escalating violence, generated by the armed confrontation between the State and the non-State forces, along with the declaration of Manipur as a 'disturbed' State, that women became significantly involved with the public and political acts. The draconian Armed Forces Special Powers Act 1958 was imposed in Manipur which empowers the Armed Forces with special immunity that goes beyond accountability and violates very fundamentals of democracy. Since then the notion of a peaceful and happy life have become just stories. Gross human rights violation in the form of illegal detentions, torture, fake encounters, extra-judicial killings, rape of women, firing on civilians, etc., have by then, become a daily affair. These new circumstances led to the change of '*Nisha Bandis*' to '*Meira Paibis*' (women torch bearers), and they rose into prominence as the most powerful defenders of human rights against any form of repression and violence.

Motherhood rhetoric and Gendered Resistances

A significant attribute of the *Meira Paibis* is that, unlike in any other violence prone societies, these women became the 'protectors' in a highly patriarchal setting. The traditionally stable power equation shook a little as we see the 'original' protector, men, becoming the 'protected'. The withering of the 'sexual contract', borrowing Carole Pateman's term, is unfortunately not caused by some long drawn struggle for equality and empowerment by women and like-minded men, but through situation-induced, optionless, violent socio-political circumstances, whereby men became equally vulnerable. So these women, to accomplish their newly deputed role, spend nights outside their homes, patrolling their local streets. Sacrificing their own comforts, they guard their families from any surprise assault of the army and the state commandoes. Their *Meira* (torch) is not just a source of light, but also a companion, a guide, which gives a sense of security and simultaneously their only weapon.

The escalation of violence incited the motherly dimensions among the *Meira Paibis*. They have been vigilant throughout, striking back at the State for every abuse it commits. The Langjing massacre (1980), Heirangoithong Massacre (1984), Oinam Massacre (1987), Tera bazar Massacre (1993), RIMS Massacre (1995), the Malom Massacre (2000), and many more, still haunt the lives of the people of Manipur. The Meira Paibis and their efforts in securing the release of Lourembam Ibomcha in the Maibam leikai incident (1980), and the subsequent marking of *Pari Kanba Numit*,[4] is still regarded by many as the birth of the Meira Paibi movement. Among the many cases relating to 'enforced disappearances' the arrest of the 14-year old High School Board examinee became epochal. Yumlembam Sanamacha Singh from Angtha Mayai Leikai, Imphal East, was preparing for his forthcoming Board examinations when he was picked up on the night of 12 February 1998. It was around 11 p.m., that he and two other boys were taken away by the 17 Rajputana Rifles (RR). While the other two boys were released the following day, the whereabouts of Sanamacha is still not known. The 17 RR denied the charges that they picked up the student and it was only after a long procedure of enquiry that the charges were proven. The missing of Sanamacha caused massive public hue and cry. The whole State was paralysed and was in turmoil for several months. The case of Sanamacha is still pending along with many other similar cases of 'enforced disappearances'. Besides these, the custodial rape and torture of Maibam Naobi, the extra-judicial execution of Chungkham Sanjit and Thockchom Rabina on 23rd July 2009 by Manipur police commandoes, etc. are some of the very recent gruesome acts that had ravaged the tiny State. It is against all these unabated human rights violation that the struggle of the *Meira Paibis* can be perceptively located.

In almost all cultural contexts, according to Cynthia Enloe, mothers are viewed as caretakers of even adult sons, endowed with the moral authority and sense of obligation to protect their sons and increasingly daughters from war and violence (Enloe 2000 cited in Volo 2004, 716). In the cases mentioned above and in all other cases, mothers have always been at the forefront of public protest. Their act of protest is the manifestation of the ethics of care and love associated with motherhood, transformed into an immense power of female ferocity every time injustice and oppression occur. They come out on the streets as mothers and wives against the government, seeking restoration of their missing sons and husbands. They act as a shield, and negotiate with the security forces and the militants, for the safety of their loved ones. Their fights are exemplary, demanding justice for every one tortured or killed, with an unfettered perseverance. All these conjunctures lay bare their effort to reassert the motherly virtue of nurturing life.

The demand for restoration of their disappeared sons, or their protest against killings of their husbands and sons can also be seen in a slightly different light. 'Give back my son' or 'give back my husband' are some of the very common slogans used. By taking away their sons, these women claim to have been robbed off their role of motherhood. Thus, their struggle is also an attempt to claim back their lost role. According to Malathi de Alwis, writing in the context of the mother's movement against enforced disappearances in Sri Lanka, these women's only demand was for a climate where they can raise their sons to manhood, have their husbands with them leading a normal woman's life. They claimed to have an authentic and unquestionable grief which espoused traditional family values (De Alwis 2009, 84). Ironically the State had always valourised motherhood and the notion of family, being obliged to guard and preserve it. It is this hypocritical nature of the State—both valorising and destroying the family simultaneously—that has induced these 'mothers' and 'wives', whose (inalienable) right have been slaughtered, to fight for justice. Therefore it is a fight for their rights which motherhood had endowed them with.

Redefining the 'Political'

The activism of the *Meira Paibis* speaks one language and that is the language of 'motherhood', bringing maternal care into the domain of the political. Their act of care is seen to be used as an idiom of protest. As Samir Kumar Das has pointed out, "the language these women spoke was the stereotypical women's language—the language of love, loyalty, care, and affection, but this they speak with a public anger in a public place in ways they never meant to do" (Das 2008, 70-1). The language of intimacy which belong to the non-public domain, assumed a different form when it is expressed in public, though their actions are extensions of the same role they perform in the private space when they nurture life. The language of care and nurture associated with motherhood becomes the most handy and abundant tool available to these women.

The constant use of the language of motherhood in their struggle also challenged the paradigm of motherhood as a private enclave. The loss they suffered and the pain it occasioned, pulled them out to take public action, transferring them from being biological mothers to becoming political mothers. In this transition, they manage to give new meanings and value to their traditional role. Protesting against the harm done to their children and to them as mothers, they challenged the *status quo* and developed a different political consciousness out of their experiences of suffering. The women, according to Schirmer, started using 'the language of sacrifice and the traditional values associated with motherhood as both political protection and political tools, these women are willing to take public action' (Schirmer 1989, 4). To their advantage, the image of a mother also protected them from extreme violent repression of the State, as motherhood is loaded with a moral high-ground and authority. Making full use of this aspect, the mothers question the notion of the 'political' itself by creating a space for themselves entirely based on feminine virtues. Thus their protests based on maternal care opened new avenues of participation.

Motherhood and the Denunciation of Sexuality

As has been pointed out earlier, the State's violence never distinguished between 'innocent' and 'insurgents', they also did not make any gender difference. In fact women get an extra score of violence by getting raped before they are killed. The most extraordinary incident that rocked Manipur was when the mutilated bullet ridden body of a 32 years old Thangjam Manorama was found dumped. She was picked up by the 17 Assam Rifles (AR) from her home, on 10 July 2004 around midnight, on the ground of her alleged link with the People's Liberation Army (PLA) of Manipur. Her mutilated body clearly showed that she suffered sexual violence and was later killed, with bullet signs on her private parts indicating the motive of the perpetrators to remove the evidence of rape. This incident was not one which can be forgotten easily with the passage of time. The people's long suppressed agony, and rage against the violation of life and liberties exploded.

The incident unleashed massive protests across different sections of the civil society among which the historic one was led by the *Meira Paibis*. Tired of several unheard protests, they felt that it was the right time to strike hard with an alternative mode that would strongly affirm that they cannot take the abuse any longer. The *imas* (mothers) were agonised over the inhuman beastly violence and terrified about the future of all young girls and boys. The whole world shook when these mothers (12 of them) protested naked in front of *Kangla,* then the Headquarters of the 17 Assam Rifles. The inhuman rape and killing of Thangjam Manorama was taken as a virtual rape of the entire folk, a mark of imperial power's foul play and a racial offensive. Their slogan 'Indian army rape us' spread like a wild fire, and became the most visible symbol of Manipuri women's protest worldwide. They shouted, 'We are all Manorama's mothers', 'Come take our flesh', defying the narrow boundaries of class, ethnicity and blood, freeing themselves from the specific biological context of mother-child relationship and its associated obligations. The loss which is specific to one individual or family is converted to a public cause thereby blurring the line between the two. Driven by the common concern of all people, the mothers care for all victims regardless of whose children they are. The association of mother and child is thus broadened up to an extent that every woman becomes a mother in the real or potential sense. The inherent attributes of motherhood enabled these women to treat every child as her own child, as manifested in the case of the disappeared and victimised. Thus we can see motherhood, being defined not only by the existence of an either biological or adopted child, but also maintained in the absence of the child (in cases of enforced disappearances and killed). Deconstructing the association of motherhood with biological birth, it gave rise to a new dimension in the mother-child relationship.

The nude protest also throws light into certain areas of sexuality and motherhood, occasionally seen to be conflicting. Their nudity can be explained as an act of total denunciation of sexuality and shame associated with one's body. This came along with the reassertion of motherhood, ferocious and infuriated, unable to bear the injuries caused to their sons and daughters. Both these two phenomena are contradictory as motherhood is so infused with male dominance that denunciating sexuality becomes almost impossible. But this protest seems to encompass both. The ideal image of a mother is not of a sexual erotic body; rather it is the source of life, love, care, nurture. She is bountiful and benevolent, affectionate and forgiving. So it is when this ideal image break free of all decency and morality associated with the body, that it becomes the most impossible task of even the most powerful to counter them. This act of protest is simultaneously an act of shamming the 'violator' by the 'violated'.

The act of motherhood going to the extreme of even stripping themselves reflects the very uselessness or the superficiality of clothing when the human dignity is already lost. In the words of Samir Kumar Das 'it shows the "superfluity" of their clothes' (Das 2008, 68). The female body is engraved with a lot of meanings and values, and nudity signifies that they have nothing more to lose. When this female body is that of a mother, then it becomes all the more problematic. An act of total defiance of the norms, and male glory, these mothers debunked the sexual differential mark of the ultimate 'what can only happen to women' (Spivak 1981, 388). They showed for real that the so-called male glory which had so far succeeded in unclothing women, are helpless when it comes to clothing them. Contrary to the female body, the male body is debarred of these associations with shame, morality and virtues. Little did the male protestors of the Manipur People's Party Youth Front know, that their bodies did not carry any meanings, when they protested nude (Huyen Lanpao, December 3, 2011). For them it is nothing more than being naked.

Feminism: Agency and Motherhood.

The movement of the *Meira Paibis* is also interesting in the sense that it is an organization of women but not exclusively for women. They mainly use their identities as wives and mothers in their struggle. Motherhood, thus, possesses legitimate power to mobilise and frame women's activism but, when it comes to the deconstruction of patriarchy it stops short, as the very identity of 'wife' and 'mother' only reinforces practices of male order. Doubtful about the use of idiom of motherhood to mobilise women for feminist activism, Patricia Jeffery is of the view that motherhood embeds women in the family and derives their identities from relationship and duty to others, giving little space for free decision making and agency. Further, there are notions of bearing legitimate children for their husband to preserve racial purity, combined with the idea of women as reproducers and transmitters of authentic culture. Also not to forget motherhood as an icon of national honour, that goes on to glorify nation as woman. Due to all these complexities, the use of the idiom of motherhood for movements, according to Jeffery, could actually create a separation between women (Jeffery 1998, 225). Though women's activism in Manipur is far from using religious overtones, the notion of bearing legitimate children, racial purity, and authenticity of culture does exist. But regardless of all these shortcomings, their mobilisation based on feminised repertoires did create a space for themselves where they could assert their voices. They fill in new meanings and dimensions to their traditional role on the one hand, and also hitherto unfamiliar components in the public realm. Rita Manchanda, while studying the role of women in peace activism, has also pointed out that women in their everyday activities of managing survival politicised their reproductive and nurturing roles. Their political activity is driven by the everyday reality they face, and they do it to assert the safety of their family. The creation of a public space for themselves through their activism is thus, quite a liberating experience for ordinary women (Manchanda 2001, 52).

The invocation of motherhood in their protest should be seen as a wise tactic rather than simply a reinforcement of old order. It provides women with one of the few entry points to organise and assert themselves. Using the metaphor of motherhood is advantageous to women, as mothers are assumed to be 'apolitical' creatures and, therefore, not dangerous. It is also more acceptable and legitimate, more likely to gain sympathy because it is seen as an extension of women's traditional role. They have the moral weight in their fight and their political messages and demands have profound impact, which are difficult to refute. They came out on the streets when their men, who are the traditional protectors, failed to accomplish their role due to the prevailing atmosphere of fear and insecurity. Their identity of mother makes them able to counter any form of powerful authority. It is precisely at this time that their struggle for everyday survival, and their concern for the safety of their family, became a political act. The concern for their loved ones, the love, care and protection, their ability to reproduce and preserve life, all get entwined in the struggle of the *Meira Paibis*. They guard their sons and daughters, family and community from any possible harm. They let the virtues of motherhood flow freely, and it is when they were not allowed to do so that they came out in protest. Rather than giving in to sufferings, they have fought with their unhealed wounds. Battling against all kinds of atrocities and crimes, the *Meira Paibis* have made their own mark in history. Their strength and vigour should not be subverted. They should not allow themselves to be misled and used. They should be firm and clear with their goals and orientations, as they have the power to save the youth and the society, free its women from the shackles of tradition and backwardness. This women power should be well harvested and preserved.

NOTES

1. The rise of new Assisted Reproductive Technologies (ARTs) such as *in vitro* fertilization, artificial insemination, etc., promises a solution for infertility to individuals and couples who are unable to reproduce the natural way. Interestingly the reproduction process has become more perplex, with conflicting issues and interests.
2. *Meira Paibi* literally means women torch bearer. *Meira* which signifies light, is an improvised bamboo torch. More than a source of light, it is an identification of confidence, security, dignity and moral strength.
3. *Nupi Lan* literally translated as women's agitation or women's war is significant in the history of Manipur. The first *Nupi Lan* was a result of the British introduction of new colonial administrative system including the abolition of 'Lallup system' (a kind of feudal system). They challenged the economic policies of the British that had caused economic exploitation of the state by outside traders. Second *Nupi Lan* is a direct protest against rice hoarding by the Marwari traders despite scarcity of rice in the valley which is coupled with the maladministration of the British. See, N Joykumar Singh, 2005, *Social Movements in Manipur,* 73-94.
4. *Pari* (son) and *Kanba* (save) would mean the 'safeguarding of sons'. Therefore with *Numit* meaning Day, *Pari Kanba Numit* is the day when they were able to successfully save their son from the jaws of death. The incident was triggered by the arrest of Ibomcha, a resident of Tomal Makhong, Liwa Road Singjamei, on grounds of suspicion, following a plantation of three bombs by the insurgents in the area. The local women folks along with some members of the All Manipur Women's Reformation and Development Samaj, secured the release of Ibomcha and since then, the day i.e., 29th December of every year is commemorated as the Pari Kanba Numit every year.

REFERENCES

Arendell, Terry, (Nov., 2000). 'Conceiving and Investigating Motherhood: The Decade's Scholarship', *Journal of Marriage and Family*, Vol. 62, No. 4 pp. 1192-1207, URL: http://www.jstor.org/stable/1566731 Accessed: 22/02/2010 02:17.

Chenoy, M. Anuradha, 2001. *Millitarism and Women in South Asia*. New Delhi: Kali for Women.

De Alwis, Malathi, 2009. 'Interrogating the 'political': Feminist Peace Activism in Sri Lanka', *Feminist Review*,9.

Das, Samir Kumar, (2008), *Ethnicity and Democracy meet when Mothers Protest*. In, Women in Peace Politics, South Asian Peace Studies, Vol. 3, Paula Banerjee (eds.). New Delhi: Sage Publications.

Dutta, Anuradha and Ratna Bhuyan (ed.). 2008. *Women and Peace, Chapters from North-East India.* New Delhi: Akansha Publishing House.

Huyen Lanpao, Dec. 3, 2011. *MPP YF stages nude protest.*

Krishnaraj, Maithreyi. 2010. *Motherhood in India: Glorification without Empowerment.* New Delhi: Routledge.

Manchanda, Rita (ed.). 2001. *Women, War and Peace in South Asia: Beyond Victimhood to Agency.* New Delhi: Sage Publications.

Patricia, Jeffery. 1998. *Agency, Activism and Agendas.* In Appropriating Gender, Women's Activism and Politicized in South Asia, ed. Patricia, Jeffery and Amrita Basu, 221-244. London and New York: Routledge.

Ruddick, Sara, 1998. *Women of Peace* in Lorentzen and Turpin (eds), The Women and War Reader. New York: New York University Press.

Ruddick,Sara, 1980. Maternal Thinking, *Feminist Studies*, Vol. 6, No. 2., pp. 342-367, URL: http://www.jstor.org/stable/3177749 Accessed: 21/05/2010 06:53

SAMA. 2006. *ARTs and Women: Assistance in Reproduction and Subjugation.* New Delhi: Sama-Resource Group for Women and Health.

Schirmer, Jennifer G. Summer-1989. Those Who Die for Life Cannot Be Called Dead: Women and Human Rights Protest in Latin America, *Feminist Review*, No. 32, pp. 3-29. URL: http://www.jstor.org/stable/1395361, Accessed: 09/02/2010 05:00.

Singh, N. Joykumar, 2005. *Social Movements in Manipur.* Delhi: Mittal Publication.

Spivak, Gayatri Chakravorty, (Winter, 1981). 'Draupadi by Mahashveta Devi', *Critical Inquiry*, Vol. 8, No. 2, pp. 381-402, URL: http://www.jstor.org/stable/1343169, Accessed: 27/10/2010 02:21.

Volo, Lorraine Bayard de, Dec-2004. Mobilizing Mothers for War: Cross-National Framing Strategies in Nicaragua's Contra War, *Gender and Society*, Vol. 18, No. 6, pp. 715-734,URL: http://www.jstor.org/stable/4149391 Accessed: 22/02/2010 02:38.

11

Resisting the 'Other': Ethnographic Exploration of the *Lai Haraoba* in the Contemporary[1]

Rekha Konsam

Introduction

In the drawing room of my grandfather's house hung a framed black and white photograph of my aunt. She was dressed as the goddess Durga with ten hands seated on a 'lion'. The photograph was taken in the year 1977. The occasion was the event of the *Lai Haraoba* at the *umanglai* shrine in the neighbourhood. The speciality of the event was that it was the revival of the festival at this shrine after a long time. It had been held after such a long time that in recollective accounts, it is often refered to as the first time – hyphenated with the words 'since we have known'. The shrine complex that had deteriorated to a dilapidated condition had been revamped in the previous year. A new concrete structure now stood in its place. The neighbourhood had joined together heartily to make the festival a success. Young people had got together in groups to participate in different presentation. The photograph was a part of the memory of the local *Lai Haraoba* on the event of its revival in the year 1977.

The photograph was an artefact from a past that saw the 'resurrection' of the *Lai Haraoba* festival. It was a time when the contest between the revivalist movement and the Hindu Mahasabha had intensified. The revivalist movement gathered strength in the struggle to secure the image of *Lainingthou Sanamahi* from the temple of a Brahmin family in 1975 (Bijoykumar Singh 2005, 132). It was later on to start a wave of cultural reawakening amongst the masses that sought to celebrate the pre-Hindu roots that had been subdued in the wake of a flourishing Hindu culture. More importantly, the photograph is a standing testimony of a time when the Hindu goddess found a place in a *Lai Haraoba* festival. This merits special attention in the light of the *Lai Haraoba* festival in contemporary times. In May 2010, during the course of my fieldwork, local dailies carried news of a person who had been apprehended for participating in a Lai Haraoba in the garb of the Hindu god Mahadeva. This had generated discussions about the place of 'Mahadeva' in contemporary *Lai Haraoba*.

Taking the above cited cases, the article argues that while the *Lai Haraoba* is a neighbourhood social space, it is also responsive to contestations of cultural discourses that are located beyond the neighbourhood. This contestation addresses two aspects of the Meitei cultural identity, *viz.*, the Hindu and the pre-Hindu. The former seeks to explain the festival within a frame of reference that is distinctly located as a part of the Hindu universe while for the later, the *Lai Haraoba* is significant as epitomising the Meitei cultural traditions that existed prior to the State institutionalisation of Hinduism.

The festival of *Lai Haraoba* is held in honour of the *umanglai* deities at shrines dedicated to these deities. These shrines are spread out across the Meitei settlement. The festival is observed in these dispersed neighbourhood sites. As a ritual, it is a public ritual that involves the resident community but is at the same time orchestrated through the institutionalised structure of ritual specialisation. It engages the services of the three lines of ritual specialisation – the *maiba* (priest cum medicine man), the *maibi* (priestess cum midwife) and the *pena* (an indigenous musical instrument). The festival is well known for its elaborate dance rituals performed by the *maibi*s. In discursive practices, the *Lai Haraoba* has always been upheld as keeping alive the essence of the uniqueness of the Meitei ethnic people. It is upheld as an inspiration of a glorious past and an aspect that remained relatively untouched by the influence of Hinduism. It has, hence, been remarked as 'the most authentically Meitei of all the traditional festivals' and one that most closely 'preserves the ancient Manipuri culture' (Paratt 1980, 53). It 'represents the heart of the Meitei culture' and is the 'greatest single key to Meitei history and culture' (Parratt and J. Parratt 1997, vii & xiv). It "mirrors the entire culture of the Manipuri people" (Singh 1982, 36–7).

In recent times there has been concerted effort to focus attention to the festival at the level of practice. This was a response to several factors. Rather than addressing these factors, the paper proposes to focus on one of them – the articulation of a self-conscious Meitei cultural identity. In this articulation, it is not so much a question of what constitutes it but, significantly, what does *not* constitute it. It is thus a resistance against an over-arching Hindu cultural influence which comes to constitute this cultural 'other'. The appearance of the 'Mahadeva' and his consequent 'detention' is significant as an ethnographic moment of rupture. It brings to the fore certain underlying notions that reflect on the changing conception of the neighbourhood *Lai Haraoba* space. Here we explore this space as a self-conscious space for the articulation of a Meitei cultural identity. As a subject of enquiry, the *Lai Haraoba* challenges any researcher. The present exploration is limited as it seeks to address only certain aspects.

Conceptual Framework

The juxtapositioning of 'our culture' *vis-à-vis* 'other culture' goes a long way in the history of the discipline of Sociology as experienced in India. It provided a line of demarcation between the twin disciplines of Sociology and Anthropology where the former is characteristically defined as the study of 'our' culture while the later is the study of 'other' cultures (Srinivas 1987). The delineation was problematised with the growing number of scholars from these 'other' cultures who were trained in the West but sought to study their own societies. For these scholars, what constituted 'our' society in the experiential clashed with the treatment of the same as 'other' as a field of study. While the debate is a long drawn one and it is not the purpose of this essay to dwell on it, it brings to mind the fluidity of the notions of 'our' culture *vis-à-vis* 'other' cultures. The juxtapositioning was premised on the grounds of varying standpoints of scholars and their fields of study.

In the politics of identity, this juxtapositioning has an altogether different dynamics. Identity is not perceived as one, but multiple (Oomen 1997). It could be gender, nationality, race, class, and so on and so forth. Depending on time, place and situation, one identity gets prominence over another. Within the carved out space of the *Lai Haraoba* festival in Manipur, it is the two aspects of cultural identity that is brought into prominence – the Hindu and the pre-Hindu. The flourishing culture brought forth by Hinduization since the eighteenth century had come to the point where it threatened to push into oblivion the culture that pre-existed it. Revivalism sought to reclaim the tradition and identity that had been suppressed in the process of Hinduization. In the course of its development, the movement started off as anti-Bengali, anti-Brahmin and later on became anti-Hindu. The movement was not unaffected by other events taking shape. The revivalist movement was responsive to the regional political milieu. The political discontent with the Indian State added another dimension to the movement as a force of socio-political change (Bijoykumar Singh 2005, 129 & 234).

The revivalist vehemently dissociated from what they saw as distinctly influenced by Hindu culture. Although revivalism was gathering strength, it continued to be seen as being reactionary for the non-revivalists for whom the dissociation seemed blurry. The revivalist attempt to go back to a certain past was embroiled in its immediate political milieu. The blurry boundaries whereby it sought to demarcate itself from its 'other' was called to question by critics of the movement. It is interesting to posit the movement within the pan-Indian context of Hinduism as a public religion. The twentieth century emergence of Hinduism unequivocally associates itself with the Indian tradition at large by presenting itself as a universal religion (Dalmia and Von Stietencon 1995, 27). Hindu nationalism and the articulation of monolithic Hinduism threatened multiplicity within Hinduism as well as other folk religions. The experience of revivalism and its aftermath can also be seen as a response of a smaller religio-cultural entity to that of a larger one that is seen as being actively supported by the State.

The memory of oppression under which Hinduism was introduced in Manipur worked as a paradigm in the sense that uses the term as providing a narrative plot on which to contextualise a course of action

(Fisher 1980, 13 & 18). In his work based on Iran, he contends that the martyrdom of Imam Husayn serves as a paradigm. It is an 'ever-present, latent, political potential to frame or to clothe contemporary discontents'. This he refers to as the Karbala paradigm. The violence of oppression that came along with instituting Hinduism in a sense works as a paradigm. It keeps alive the memory of a new 'imported' religion that had been imposed at the cost of the 'indigene' religion which was suppressed. The revivalist movement started off as a movement to regenerate the pre-Hindu faith but it soon moved beyond that. "… [T]he primary goal of the Sanamahi movement is to restore the pre-Hindu Meitei scripts, custom, culture, and religious practices and beliefs. In other words, it aims at the de-Hinduization of Meitei socio-cultural identity and history" (Bijoykumar Singh 2005, 130).

The paradigm remained an important point of reference in the reinstating of the indigene identity.It reached out beyond the period when a flourishing Hindu influence had reached a stage where it was seen as threatening to subsume the culture that existed before it. The *Lai Haraoba* as an icon is an extension of the paradigm. It represented in a nutshell the worldview that lay at the core of the Meitei cosmology predating the 'other' cultural influence. The icon carried with it the scar of suppression that came with the institutionalisation of the Hindu religion. Not only were its related scriptures burnt in public, but several images of *umanglai* deities had been buried. It had also lost active institutional patronage.

Iconic, as it were, the *Lai Haraoba* cannot be reduced only to a religious event or to the politics of identity articulation. It is also a neighbourhood social space where entertainment forms an integral part. The physicality of the *Lai Haraoba* ground is thus a space where the dynamics of a neighbourhood public unfolds in a space accorded through a religious event and popularised in the reclamation of an authentic indigene identity. It is thus a fertile ground for the meeting and contesting of various currents. This is a characteristic feature of a public space – a space that belongs to no one but to everyone, and because it belongs to everyone it is also open to contestations. The public space of the *Lai Haraoba* is, however, a Meitei public space. This is a space where the social dynamics of a local neighbourhood comes to play with the currents located beyond the neighbourhood. In other words, the dispersed localised *Lai Haraoba* of the neighbourhood at another level constitutes a part of a single whole as 'the' *Lai Haraoba*. This whole is a subsuming over-arching ideal. In contrast to the spatial locatedness of the neighbourhood sites, 'the' *Lai Haraoba* operates more like an ideal. It is not contextualised or delimited to the particularity of a physical space but it locates itself through practice in the neighbourhood sites. Within this over-arching ideal, resistance is expressedly along the lines of what does *not* form a part of 'our' culture rather than what does form a part of it. This 'our' culture is expressedly the Meitei ethnic 'indigene' pre-Hindu identity *vis-à-vis* the 'imported' other Hindu culture. The paradigm of violence associated with the advent of Hinduism serves as a reminder of the cultural 'other' which needs to be resisted within the space of the iconic festival.

Background

In the eighteenth century, the Meitei society was introduced to Hinduism by King Pamheiba (1708-1747 AD). This introduction was not a harmonious one; rather, it was one of oppression and suppression. In the process of introducing the new religion, the older unnamed religion that had grown organically with its people had been suppressed and its adherents persecuted. People were forced to convert. Those who refused to comply were excommunicated or exiled. Several of its ritual specialists were persecuted and its scriptural texts destroyed in public.

The memory of this oppressive past remains alive. In the historical turn of events, Hinduism was popularised during the reign of King Bhagyachandra who strategically made appeal to aesthetics. His reign was the start of a flourishing Manipuri Vaishnavism where Hinduism was localized with a distinctive local flavour. This was the period that saw the birth of the Manipuri *Raslila*. It was a product of this synthesis and epitomised Manipuri Vaishnavism. It was based on the tenth Canto of the *Raas Panchadhyaya* of *Srimadbhagavad*, but structured as per the pre-Hindu ritual performance of *Lai Haraoba* (Lokendro, personal interview) and expressed through local aesthetics.[2]

The new religion was oriented, not to the immediacy of its own surroundings but to the source of its origin that lay elsewhere. Its deities, language and script were different. Its chief patrons were the elites (Chaki-Sircar 1984, 104 & 109). As Manipuri Vaishnavism flourished, the pre-Hindu religion and the culture associated with it was pushed to the periphery. It came to constitute the 'other' from which distance had to be maintained. Excommunication and social ostracism were some of the instruments to maintain the Hindu 'self'. In contrast to the Meitei experience of Hinduism that came to be associated with oppression, it was not a religion that was open to everyone. Those who accepted Vaishnavism formed a higher status category compared to the latter (Saha 1994, 34). There are also suggestions that the experience of the neighbouring ethnic communities was one of denial and hence of exclusion as conversion to Hinduism was restricted to them through the payment of a heavy tax.

The revivalist movement brought in its wake a reawakening of the pre-Hindu indigene aspect. It sought to bring back what existed prior to Hinduization in the search for an authentic Meitei indigene identity. Along with the wave, came the revival of its own script indigenous Manipuri script (*Meitei Mayek*) *vis-à-vis* the new script that had come to be in force along with Hinduization. The revivalist laid claim to the neglected aspect of the Hindu Meitei society – its pre-Hindu 'tribal' roots. It countered the claim of the Hindu society epicentred through the Hindu Mahasabha and pitched it against its own claim of being the 'authentic' 'indigenous' that was organically tied up with the people and its land. Thus, in its own discourses, the revivalist pitted itself as the 'indigenous self' which was counterposed with the 'borrowed Hindu other'.

The claims and counter-claims paradoxically bring out the ambiguity in the contesting discourses wherein the revivalist movement is seen as reactionary in character. It was a reaction to the two and a half century process of Hinduization (Bijoykumar Singh 2005, 130). Despite its characteristic reactionary mode, what it did succeed in was to generate an interest in the 'indigene'—'our' culture— the culture of the forefathers' *vis-à-vis* the 'other' culture. Beyond the revivalist discourse, it led to an avowed revival of the pre-Hindu aspects amongst the general masses. Folk songs gained popularity as also the observance of festivals as per the pre-Hindu calendar (Ibemu Devi 1991, 153–56). Naming pattern changed with increasing preference to opt for 'Meitei' names—a trend that seems to find favour with the growing diasporic community. Nomenclature changed with several people opting to drop the Hindu title of 'Singh'/ 'Devi' for 'Meitei'/'Chanu' or their respective clan names.[3]

The 1970's came across as a time when there was a rekindling of interest in the pre-Hindu aspects of the Meitei culture. The pre-established sites that had hosted the festival in the past started observing it once again. Correspondingly, there was also a mushrooming of the pre-Hindu public festival of *Lai Haraoba* held in honour of the *umanglai* deities. Several *umanglai* shrines bear the year of its construction in the late 1970's and early 1980's. During the course of my fieldwork, several of the shrines were in the process of being reconstructed. The new structures are increasingly more stylish and clearly commanded more resources.

The Place of 'Mahadeva' in Contemporary *Lai Haraoba*

The premise of the *Lai Haraoba* lies in a religious conception within which the *umanglai* is an integral part of the pre-Hindu Meitei cosmogony. However, it is not limited to religiosity. Representative rites and collective recreations have a close connection and man may pass from one to the other without any break of continuity. As an event unfolding in a public space, the ritual and the recreations together constitute a part of the *Lai Haraoba*.

Within the frame of reference of the Meitei 'indigenous' cultural identity, 'the' *Lai Haraoba* is constituted not only in the rituals but also finds extension into its other aspects. The line-up of performances of a non-ritual entertainment programme at any *Lai Haraoba* is generally a voluntary decision. The participants themselves decide what they would like to perform. These performances range from Manipuri dance to martial arts and acrobatics to *shumang lila* (plays performed on courtyard or open space rather than on decorated stage). In some sites, I was even told about fashion shows and cross-dressed performances. Conspicuous in these items was the absence of certain performances which otherwise were always a part of the dance itinery for any such showcasing. Be it the Manipur state tourism festival or festival for any performing arts, Manipuri dances often include a showcasing of dances from both the 'folk' or 'classical' traditions.[4]

Within the context of the present day *Lai Haraoba* festival in the neighbourhoods, one does not get to see the performance of a *pung cholom* or a *sankirtan* or the *raslila* (ritual dance and music genres associated with Hinduized Meitei community). These performances have their roots in Hindu tradition but have moved outside the fold of their religious base to secular spaces of performance and often make their appearance in stage shows. However, they are conspicuous by their absence in contemporary *Lai Haraoba* festivals. There is a sense in which these performances do not figure as part of the items that can be performed within the setting of a *Lai Haraoba*.

In the light of this divide, the news item about the apprehended 'Mahadeva' and reactions to it merit special attention. The issue was received on two fronts – (i) the task of the newly formed taskforce of *Umanglai Kanba Apunba Lup* (UKAL) who sought to police the conduct of the festival, and (ii) the idea that someone would dress up as the Hindu god 'Mahadeva' for a *Lai Haraoba*. Discussion on the second front was accompanied with an undecided anxiety – '*yabarone*'? can it be done? The undecisiveness rang from the possibility that the performance in question could perhaps have been a part of the entertainment section, but it certainly could not have been part of the religious conduct. This draws up the question; can the space of entertainment opened up by the festival be treated only as a recreational space?

Earlier works had made reference to this section as secular items (Bharucha 1998, 167-80) and secularization of the festival (Chaki-Sircar 1984). Such delineations can be read as recognition of the qualitative difference within the usage of the space. In discussions on the *Lai Haraoba*, this latter space is differentiated from the core part of the festival which remains the ritual. For the person in the neighbourhood, this space is popularly refered to as 'entertainment'. Both the ritual core and the entertainment are equally significant. In my earlier work, I had refered to this distinction as ritual and non-ritual spaces (Konsam 2005, 206-214). This was mainly keeping in mind the idea that this space for entertainment where 'secular' items are performed is very much a part of the festival itself. It is an extension of the festival beyond the ritual confines.

The idea of extension is expressed in the words of an informant, '*umanglai gi maphamda mayanglai ga mari leinaba thouram touheide*'—any conduct related to *mayanglai* is forbidden to be performed at the place of the *umanglai*. *Mayanglai* refers to the deities of the Hindu pantheon while *umanglai* belongs to the indigenous religion. The comment firstly refers to a sense of continuity in terms of the locatedness within the sphere of *umanglai*. Secondly, it refers to a sense of incompatibility. The concept of *touheidaba* is a forbiddence that has roots in religiosity. It essentially refers to incompatibility to the concept of the sacred (Durkheim 1954). Incompatibility to the profane underlies the notion of the sacred as outlined by Durkheim while for Eliade, the sacred is carved out from the sea of chaos (Eliade 1959). In this case, it is not so much an opposition of the sacred to the profane, rather an opposition within the concept of the sacred. Furthermore, it is not the opposition of bad sacred and good sacred. It is rather an opposition of two sacreds that is grounded on two different religious worlds.

The idea of incompatibility of the Mahadeva to the *Lai Haraoba* is articulated on another plane as 'unrelated to our culture' – *eikhoigi inat ka mari leinadaba*. It is thus situated on the plane of contesting discourses of what constitutes a Meitei cultural identity.

Within the politics of cultural identity, there are two aspects of the Manipuri identity—the Manipuri Vaishnava Hindu aspect and the pre-Hindu indigenous aspect. The former seeks allegiance to the Hindu land that lies to its west. As such, Manipur was the land of princess Chitrangada of the *Mahabharata* epic. It was the land of Babhruvahana, the son of Arjuna. It was also the land chosen by Mahadeva to hold his *raslila* and where the serpent Anantanag's *mani* shone bright lighting up the entire place. The place got its present name as a derivative from the later connection. This *ras* of Mahadeva was the *Lai Haraoba*. The pre-Hindu indigenous identity, on the other hand, emphasises the culture that existed prior to Hinduization, upheld as the culture and heritage of the forefathers. Within this, the *Lai Haraoba* is a beacon that holds high the shaft of the Meitei ethnic self. The festival, the religious event, the tradition – in that sense forms a whole. It is the reservoir from which was derived that exquisite Hindu performance, the Manipuri *raslila*. It was also a tradition that was oriented to the immediacy of its neighbouring ethnic communities.

Reading the absence of the Hindu-related performances in contemporary observance of the *Lai Haraoba* festival within the context of the growing self-conscious representation of the Meitei self, the former can also be perceived as an extension of the latter. The conspicuous absence of these distinctly Hindu performances in contemporary times is broken by the appearance of the 'Mahadeva'.

The undecided deliberation rather than an immediate denial can be seen as located on the premise of the *Lai Haraoba* as a space for entertainment. Theoretically there is no defined rule as to what can or cannot be a part of this space. It is a space that is open. The fact that the Mahadeva no longer has a place even as an entertainment pushes us once more to the idea that it is not only the ritual core but the non-ritual peripheral section that together constitute the *Lai Haraoba* as a locus of cultural contestation.

As such it is shaped by a need to encourage performances that are specifically related to the culture that it stands for as an icon. Thus, in one site a presentation of *Khongjomparva* sang stories of the feats of Khongjom war,[5] while at another site, there were readings of scriptural texts telling stories of Meitei deities. A performance by the Huiyen Lalong School of Martial Arts was a specially attraction at yet another site. These three presentations were made by people professionally trained artists along their lines and were special presentations in the sense that such performances are not preponderant. The local favourites remain to be the *khamba-thoibi jagoi, leima jagoi, maibi jagoi* and the *hao jagoi* (different genres of folk music and dance).

Performances distinctly related to the indigene culture are not the only items that form a part of the presentations. *Shumang lila* plays are a special attraction. Some sites included acrobatic performance. In one site, I was also told about a cross-dressed beauty contest. 'Cassette-dance' which had at one time flooded the presentations has also been discouraged. These are dances on tracks of popular songs. Although in certain places it is still performed on popular Manipuri tracks. Given the force of the contesting discourses, the persistence of such items on the one hand and resistance to certain others makes sense in terms of a resistance to that cultural 'other'.

It would not be too far-fetched to surmise that the issue is not so much directed towards preservation of an 'authentic' *Lai Haraoba* as carving out a cultural sphere of influence. Attempts towards 'preservation' of an 'authentic' tradition raises the question of what is it that constitutes the idea of 'authentic' and how far would one draw the lines of 'preservation' specially in context to a living tradition. In context to the *Lai Haraoba*, the concern is oriented primarily to resisting the cultural 'other'. This resistance is double-pronged for in resisting the cultural 'other', the dispersed neighbourhood *Lai Haraoba* festival is drawn even more closer to the contesting discourses.

Not much has been written or documented on the neighbourhood space of entertainment of the *Lai Haraoba*. In the absence of such previous records, personal photographic collections form an important point of reference to address its changing profile. The photograph cited at the beginning of this essay spoke of a time when neighbourhood observances of *Lai Haraoba* received a new leash of life in the aftermath of a growing revivalist movement. The 1970's also comes across as a fertile time in the performative traditions. Although it would be premature to make such an assumption without further reference, conversations about this period frequently make references to *Gourlila*, *Ramlila* (dance dramas associated with Hinduized Meiteis) and such performances. The imprint of these performances was reflected in the localised public space of the neighbourhood. In these spaces, it was not the specialised artiste trained in these genres but the people of the neighbourhood themselves who put up the performances under the guidance of a teacher.

The framed photograph of the enactment of Durga was not an exception. There were pictures of enactment of Shakuntala, Ram-Sita and Mahadeva dated mostly till the first-half of the 1980's. These pictures are reflective of a period when the resurgence of the *Lai Haraoba* was not necessarily seen in opposition to the distinctly Hindu sphere. It was fuelled by a sense of re-claiming that part of a tradition that had been neglected—hence, the revival of the festival. At the level of the neighbourhood, this reclamation gave sanction for a legitimate public space. The resurgence was yet to take the form of a self-conscious representation of the *Lai Haraoba* as part of contesting discourses on cultural identity wherein the neighbourhood festival is the locus for a self-conscious articulation of a Meitei 'indigene' identity.

The imposition of ban on public broadcasting of Hindi movies as well as popular Hindi music tracks in September 2000 gave impetus to the carving out of a public culture wherein certain items were consciously not to be put forth. This had implications on the *Lai Haraoba* as a public space. Along with the disappearance of the Hindu-themed performances and dance-dramas, performances on popular song tracks had gained popularity. With the ban on Hindi, these song tracks specially the ones from Hindi popular entertainment no longer found place as entertainment items. Hinduism as a cultural influence and Hindi as a language were thus constituted outside of sphere of the *Lai Haraoba*.

The undecided anxiety on the issue of the 'Mahadeva' news item was shaped by the certainty of unrelatedness in terms of cultural paradigms wherein 'Mahadeva' was a figure firmly located in the 'other' culture. Within an understanding of the functioning of the religious conduct, it further ruled out the possibility that such a figure would have anything to do with the rituals of the *Lai Haraoba per se*. This left open the possibility that the figure probably was making an appearance in the non-ritual segment that was mainly oriented towards entertainment. Having said thus, it also reflects an awareness of the present day cultural politics wherein the space of the *Lai Haraoba* has become an important arena of resisting the cultural 'other'.

Conclusion

The public space is an open space that belongs to no one. In a sense it is open to everyone and precisely because of this, it is a contested space. What happens here and what becomes visible here comes to be closely noted. It is influenced by various flows and imbued with power relations with its own dynamics of inclusion and exclusion. This space is not static rather it is dynamic, constantly changing as per changing socio-politico-economic world order. As such it remains a space that is not only constantly watched but closely contested.

The space of *Lai Haraoba* is a public space and the site for contestations of various sorts. As a localised neighbourhood space, it is open to certain social dynamics of the residential community. This same space as part of a broader cultural space of 'the' *Lai Haraoba* is the site for a different kind of contestation. It is a site where the distinctiveness of an 'indigene' Meitei cultural identity is asserted.

This assertion takes shape in a resistance against that other which threatens it. The paradigm of violence associated with the advent of this 'other' religion and its corresponding cultural influence is resisted in the space of the *Lai Haraoba* which stands tall as an icon of that indigenous 'self'.

NOTES

1. The present study is based on fieldwork conducted in and around Imphal during the course of 2008 to 2010 covering three seasons of the festival as part of my doctoral research. Observations have been based on the study of specific case study sites.
2. There are not many books which have reflected on this aspect of synthesis, but it is something that is often refered to in conversations. Some aspects are mentioned in the work of Jamini Devi. Devi, Jamini, 'Cultural History of Manipur: Sija Laioibi and the Maharas', New Delhi: Mittal Publications, 2010.
3. For an analysis of the changes in the naming patter, refer to Shobhana L. Chelliah 'Asserting Nationhood Through Personal Name Choice: The Case of the Meithei of Northeast India', in *Anthropological Linguistics*, Vol. 47, No. 2, Summer, 2005: 169-216.
4. The usage of the terms 'folk' and 'classical' here is with reference to its colloquial usage. It does not delve into the question of what each of the two terms constitute as separate categories.
5. Khongjom war was fought between the Manipuri and the British forces in the year 1891.

REFERENCES

Balibar, Etienne and Immanuel Wallerstein. 1991. *Race, Nation, Class: Ambiguous Identities*. London & New York: Verso.

Bharucha, Rustom. 1998. The Shifting Sites of Secularism. *Economic and Political Weekly*, Vol. 33, No. 4: 167-80 (Jan. 24-30).

Bijoykumar Singh, Kh. 2005. *Sanamahi Movement Among the Meiteis of Manipur—A Sociological Study of a Socio-Religious Movement*. PhD Thesis, Jawaharlal Nehru University: New Delhi.

Chaki-Sircar, Manjusri. 1984. *Feminism in a Traditional Society: Women of the Manipur Valley.* Delhi: Shakti Books.

Dalmia, V. and H. Von Stietencron (ed.) 1995. *Representing Hinduism—The Construction of Religious Traditions and National Identity*. New Delhi: Sage Publications, 1995: 27.

Durkheim, Emile. 1954. *The Elementary Forms of Religious Life*. London: Allen & Unwin.

Eliade, Mircea. 1959. *The Sacred and the Profane: The Nature of Religion*. New York & London: Harcourt Brace Jovanovich.

Fisher, Michael M.J. 1980. *Iran: From Religious Dispute to Revolution*. (Harvard Studies in Cultural Anthropology) Harvard: Harvard University Press.

Ibemu Devi, Wairokpam. 1991. *Meitei Revivalism in Manipur*. PhD Thesis, Manipur University: Imphal.

Konsam, Rekha. 2005. Lai Haraoba: Discursive Practices and Cultural Contestation. *Eastern Quarterly*. Volume 3 issue III: 206–14. October-December.

Lokendro, Arambam, *Personal Interview*.

Oomen, T.K. 1997. *Citizenship, Nationality, and Ethnicity: Reconciling Competing Identities*. New York: Polity Press.

Parratt, S.N. 1980. *The Religion of Manipur: Beliefs, Rituals and Historical Development*. Calcutta: Firma KLM (Pvt.) Limited.

Parratt, S.N.A. and J. Parratt. 1997. *The Pleasing of the Gods: Meitei Lai Haraoba*. New Delhi: Vikas Publishing House Pvt. Ltd.

Saha, Ranajit Kumar. 1994. *Valley Society of Manipur: A Cultural Frontier of Indian Civilization*. Calcutta: Punthi-Pustak.

Singh, E.N. 1982. *Aspects of Indian Culture*. Imphal: Jawaharlal Nehru Manipur Dance Academy.

Srinivas, M.N. 1987. Development of Sociology in India: An Overview. *Economic and Political Weekly*, Vol. 22, No. 4, Jan. 24. http://dilipchandra12.hubpages.com/hub/Differences-between-Sociology-and-Anthropology accessed on January 16, 2012.

12

The Kuki National Assembly

Historicity and Evolution

Sonthang Haokip

Impact of British Rule and Christianity

The British rule coupled with the coming of Christian missionaries brought tremendous political, social and religious changes in the Kuki society. The contributions of Christianity can be seen in their religious system, their social system, and their political system. Religiously, the Gospel of Christ transformed the spiritual life of the Kukis, nullified the superstitious beliefs and eradicated demonic powers among the Kuki people. In the social context, the coming of Christianity made inroads in education, economy, and transformed the tribals, in almost all aspects of life. Politically, the British rule caused great harm to the Kukis, it created a separate geographical zone of their ancestral domain in as many as three parts, never to be united again. However, the subsequent coming of Christianity and western education created political consciousness in the Kuki society that resulted in the formation of various socio-political organizations. Of the irreparable damage done to the Kukis by the imposition of colonial rule, L. Keivom states, "The greatest harm the British did to the Kukis was the trifurcation of Kuki inhabited areas into three sovereign countries namely, India, Burma (Myanmar) and East Pakistan (Bangladesh). Thus, unpardonable damage had already been done since 1935 with the passage of the bill by the British

Parliament for administrative division of India and Burma as per the Government of India Act of 1835, which become effective in 1937" (Keivom 2010).

Another Kuki scholar, T. Haokip comments, "The Indo-Burma and the Indo-Bangladesh border is inhabited by a host of Kuki ethnic communities, who were separated by the division of British India and the then Burma in 1937 and the Partition of India in 1947. These ethnic communities have more in common with the population living across the border than with their own nationals". He goes on to state that, "India and Burma followed the British delineation of the Indo-Burmese border. This artificial border has not only caused discomfort but also ruthlessly suppressed the aspiration of the Kuki ethnic people to live together under one administrative system"(Haokip 2010, 198). As such the ramifications of such policies were termed as the "British Apartheid" (Maitra and Maitra 1995). Also the closure of the borders between the North-East and the neighbouring countries since 1947 has had adverse repercussions on the economy and society. The political division of ethnic groups (including the Kuki ethnic community), the disruption of old trade routes and people-to-people contact is termed as "colonialism's most enduring negative legacy" (Baruah 2005).

North-East India consists of mosaic of cultures and ethnic groups with each ethnic group harbouring dream of making one's identity acknowledged and valued. This realization has not been developed overnight but gradually. It has taken time for the people to realise their identity and know their needs and wants. Besides, the political atmosphere too has charged itself with electrifying speed that no people are left behind in this process of political maturity. People have become conscious of their life, their rights and status. As a result they (Kukis) began to understand that politics is a medium and politicians are the tools to attain many things. Hence, politics has become stormy not only in the valley but also in the hills of Manipur. Due to this new awakening, today we find several polarities emerged in the State of Manipur (Jeyaseelan 1993, 314-15).

The formation of ethnic based political associations among the non-Naga tribes is found as early as 1946, when Kuki National Assembly (KNA) was formed with the primary objectives of building a consciousness of common identity, to cater the political interests of the Kuki people in the post-independence era, and creating a single political unit for the Kukis. The constituent tribes of Kuki National Assembly were the Thadous, Paites, Vaipheis, Gangtes, Simtes, Zous, Anals, Koms, Hmars, Guites, Chirus, Monsang, Koirengs, etc. The post-independence period witnesses the resurgence of various tribes in North-East India. The coming of Christianity and the advancement of English education led to the rise of a small middle class among the tribes and the rise of ethnic consciousness among them. With British patronage the Naga Club was formed in 1918, which was the first attempt to organise political opinion in the Naga Hills. The Kukis were not far behind in such consciousness. They were fully aware of the various aspects of the vexing problems of the hills and the valley and, therefore, pledged to be under Manipur if only conditions were satisfactory. After independence the KNA demanded a separate State for the Kukis within India. In this regard the KNA submitted several memoranda to the Central Government but it yielded no response. In pursuance of their demand for a 'Kuki State', the Kuki National Assembly sent a Memorandum to the First Prime Minister of Free India, Pandit Jawaharlal Nehru, on 24th of March, 1960, that states;

> *"The only solution for the Kuki problem is the Kuki State, where the Kukis will have their own government to take care of their needs within the Union of India. A separate State for the Kukis with Manipur as the bastion will also give them the full opportunity to attain full growth. The Kuki State, as demanded, will enable collection of the Kuki minorities elsewhere together in a place where their lives and properties can be secure and their due share of development ensured"*
> (Memorandum of KNA to PM of India, 1960).

Kuki National Assembly 1946: Socio-Political Background

The KNA, a regional political party in the hills was the product of the process for the establishment of democratic institutions and extension of franchise to Manipur on the eve of the British departure. Besides, the long sufferings and sacrifices of the Kukis (freedom fighters/patriots), the pains and the agony of their forefathers were not in vain, as similar sentiments and objectives of their forefathers become an intrinsic part of the actions of KNA in the mid-sixties. The historical background of the origin of the party could be traced back to the formation of the 'Kuki Chiefs' Association' in 1935–36. The Association demanded the abolition of "*pothang bekari*" (forced labour) and the "*pothang senkhai*" (under which each household was to give money or chicken, eggs, etc., to the touring officials) system prevalent in the hill areas of Manipur during the British period (Ray 1992, 185-86).

The British administration over the Kuki inhabited areas, as in the case of other tribes in Manipur, was indirect and for a long period the Thadou chiefs enjoyed sufficient freedom of action. But in the later part of colonial rule, the Kuki chiefs felt insecure. On the eve of independence of India and the departure of the British, the Nagas and the Lushais demanded separate homelands. The Kukis of Manipur felt the need for uniting and forming a Kuki organization for themselves to promote the interest of the Kukis (Sharma 2003, 111). As having an organization to safeguard their interest, became the need of the hour, T. Kipgen, then a C.O. (Circle Officer) convened a meeting of the Kuki chiefs, the meeting was attended by many Kuki Chiefs and other prominent members of the Kuki society. Thus, in this way the Kuki National Assembly came into being as a socio-political organization of the Kukis on October 24, 1946, at the Kuki Co-Operative Building in Imphal (Pudaite 2002, 99). T. Kipgen, imported the word, "Assembly" from the French National Assembly of the French Revolution to put into the nomenclature of the new political party (Sharma 2003, 111). The flag of the party was designed by H. Thangjom; the background green representing the "Hills", the red, "Bravery" and the star representing "Unity". The founding president and secretary of the party were S.M. Zavum and T. Kipgen respectively (Sharma 2003, 111).

In the beginning, KNA was not an active political party. It was rather a political platform of the Kuki chiefs. The party adopted its constitution on 17th October 1969 (Preamble to the Constitution of KNA, 1986). It was recognised as a "State Party" by the Election Commission of India and allotted "Two Leaves" as its symbol in 1975 (KNA Constitution, 26).

Kuki National Assembly (KNA): Its Ideology, Policy and Programme

The ideology of the KNA developed around the purview of one's love and feeling for the preservation and protection of one's own ethnic identity (Sharma 2003, 114). The party aims at uniting all the Kukis living in different States of India and to stand united by organizing themselves for a political status. The Party also expressed a strong determination to make a homeland for the Kukis. The Party further pledged to improve the living and economic conditions of the Kukis and also to improve education of the Kukis. The Annual Conference of the Kuki National Assembly which was held from 23rd to 25th October, 1946, formulated its 'Future Policy', which states,

> Taking into consideration the various aspects of the vexing problems of the hills and the valley, it is the desire of the Kuki National Assembly to announce that the Kukis should come under the Durbar provided the conditions are satisfactory, but failing to obtain satisfactory conditions, the Kukis regrètfully, will have to follow the footsteps of their hill brethren in demanding for full secession (Resolution of the Annual Kuki National Assembly Conference, 23rd to 25th October, 1946).

However, after some years of its existence, not pleased with the Thadou dominancy and supremacy, the non-Thadou tribes started searching for a more democratic organization as an alternative to the KNA. This gave birth to Khulmi National Union in 1947 with one Mr. Teba Kilong as its President and the tribes like Vaiphei, Gangte, Simte, Paite, Zou, Manlun Manchong, Kom, Chiru, Aimol, Purum, Tarao, Moyon, Anal, Maring, Baite Hrangchal, Khongsai (Lunkim, Changsan, Lhangum, Len-thang) and Saum Doungel who believed, as their folk history recorded is originated from 'Khul' meaning 'cave' became the constituent ethnic groups of the canopy term 'Khulmi'. In 1951, the unification of different tribes of the Kukis under the nomenclature of 'Khulmi', received a fatal blow as it was not granted recognition by the Government of India. The seriousness of the case was that, though the term 'Khulmi', ceased to function, none of its members returned to the Kuki fold thereafter.

Another setback to the unity of Kuki, was the formation of another term 'KOMREM', which was formed by the erstwhile Kuki tribes such as, Kom, Aimol, Chiru, Koireng, Purum, Kharam, etc. Furthermore, the so-called old Kukis of the present day Chandel District of Manipur merged into the Naga fold during 1960s. Thus, began the political disintegration of the Kuki tribes of Manipur into many splinter groups.

The new political awakening in the post-independence era however proved a great setback to the unity and oneness of the Kuki family (Vaiphei 1975, 58-59). The consciousness of their separate identity led them to ask the Government for recognition of their tribe. As a result, tribes and clans which have been within the Kuki fold, one after another sought and get their respective tribe/clan recognition as a separate entity, which marked the beginning of the Kuki fragmentation as a great nation. In this regard, Gangte remarks,

> In the past, till the end of British rule in India, different ethnic groups did not object to being identified as Kuki when inter-tribal feuds were the practice of the time. The term 'Kuki' gave security and protection, and was an expression of solidarity and identity. After independence the Constitution of India provides special provisions for growth and development of the weaker sections of the people. These groups no longer feel the necessity of being called 'Kuki'. They feel that they should avail to the fullest extent possible of the privilege being accorded to them by the Constitution of India (Gangte 1993, 231).

As a result many political organizations based on narrow ethnic lines, which were splinter groups of Kuki National Assembly (KNA), *viz.*, the Hmar Congress (1954), and the Hmar National Union (1962), the Paite National Council (1956), the Gangte Tribe Union (1958) emerged in the political scenario of the Kukis (Chaube 1973, 195). Thus, the ground was set for a multitude of other splinter groups to mushroom. Assertion of smaller identities against the collective one became the pattern. The constitution of Tribe Modification Order 1956 reinforced these identities, keeping the Kuki identity at risk.

Even before India's independence, the Kuki National Assembly started putting strong pressure for a satisfactory solution concerning land alienation problem of the Kukis, abolition of the forced labour system and the grant of equal rights with the plainsmen, the hill representatives in the Assembly (Manipur) be nominated by the hill people, etc. (Resolution of the KNA, Working Committee, 1947) Though the KNA was not in a position to materialise the dream of the Kukis for a homeland, it became a forerunner of the future Kuki Movements for an amicable solution to the Kuki problems.

The history of Kuki National Movements (relating to the Kukis of Manipur) may be classified into two phases: (1) KNA Period, 1946-1980s and, (2) Post-KNA periods, from 1980s onwards. The former may be compared as the Moderate Phase of the India National Congress and the latter as that of the Extremist era. During the former era, the Kuki national leaders have firm belief in the sincerity of the Government of Free India; it sent memorandums, petitions and other peaceful mechanisms so that their plights are look into. As a result of ignorance in spite of utilizing peaceful methods, the year from 1980 onwards marked the coming up of Kuki insurgency movements fighting for bringing an amicable solution to the Kuki problems which have long been ignored.

Growth of Kuki Armed Movements in 1980s

The Kukis were in dilemma in the post-independence era, as their future status as a nation was at stake, coupled with the merger of Manipur to the Union of India in 1949. The States in independent India are organised on linguistic lines giving due recognition to languages and culture of a community. However, the Kukis argue that this right to govern their affairs within their 'traditional territory' has been denied to them, while it has long been granted to other major ethnic groups in the North-East India. The demands of the Kukis for the creation of a 'Kuki State' within the framework of Constitution of India in the 1960s nor the creation of Kuki dominated Sadar Hills into a full-fledged district in the 1970s and 1980s through a peaceful means have not been acknowledged both by the Manipur and Central governments (Haokip 2010, 5).

The measures adopted by the colonialists, such as the setting up of administrative posts in Tamenglong and Ukhrul (in favour of the Nagas) to displace the original Kuki bases of Laijang and Chassad, have been continued by the successive Manipur and Central governments. While the District Councils dominated by the Nagas were upgraded into full-fledged districts soon after Manipur attained statehood in 1972, the Kuki dominated District Councils of Tengnoupal and Sadar Hills had been left out. In 1982, the State Cabinet decided to grant full-fledged district status to Sadar Hills but failed to carry it through, and successive governments, have also failed to keep their promise. The Kukis claim that they have been subjected to political adversity and that their neighbouring communities have taken advantage of their consequent vulnerability. The aspirations of the Kukis for self-determination through peaceful means have been conveniently ignored. The only response they get is repression, deprivation and further discrimination (Haokip 2010, 6-7).

The creation of new States in North-East India and the overlook of the Kukis' demand for "Kuki-land" (State) have hurt the sentiment of the Kukis which resulted in alienation and marginalization to a great extent from mainstream India. Having witnessed and experienced the step-motherly attitude and treatment from the Government of India for many decades since India's independence, the young generations of the late eighties pledged to take up arms and resolved to fight until a separate State for the Kukis is carved out (Kipgen 1993). This, in their assessment, was the only viable strategy to pressurise the Government of India. Thus, the formation of a revolutionary organization was nothing new nor was it an accident; rather it is a continuation of the unfulfilled works which had long been started by their predecessors in the mid 1960s. The disparity between the earlier Kuki National Assembly and the present revolutionary groups can be compared to that of the moderates and the extremists in the erstwhile pre-independence India. Though there may be variations in their approach and ideology, their objectives however, remain the same. Thus, the formation of a revolutionary organization appears as fulfilments of a long-awaited cherish dream and desire of all Kuki people, men and women, the educated, the rich and the poor and the like.

Thus, the wait for an amicable solution to the 'Kuki issue' from the side of the Central government becoming just a dream, the Kukis under these circumstances, were compelled to take up armed movements as a means to settle their future status as a nation, which resulted in the formation of various Kuki armed groups since 1980s.

The Kuki National Organization (KNO) and its armed wing Kuki National Army (KNA) were formed on February 24, 1988, (Thomsong 2005) to uphold, "the right of the Kukis to govern their own affairs within a defined territory (Statehood)" one part in India and another in Burma (Myanmar). During the same year, on May 18, the Kuki National Front (KNF) was formed under the leadership of Mr. Nehkholun Kipgen at Molnoi village (Myanmar) (Kipgen, Nehlun, *Shillong Times*, 1993) to secure a separate 'Kuki State' within the Union of India by integrating all Kuki-inhabited areas of Ukhrul, Tamenglong, Chandel and Churachandpur districts and Sadar Hills sub-divisions of Senapati district of Manipur (S. Gangte, a Monograph). In the 1990s, the Kuki Defence Force (KDF) and Chin-Kuki Revolutionary Force (CKRF) were formed in different areas of Manipur by the Kukis to protect themselves and their properties from the raids of Naga militants. The Kuki Liberation Army (KLA)/Kuki Liberation Organization (KLO), was also formed to fight for a separate 'Kuki State' as its objective. (Haokip 2010, 8)

Within a couple of years of their formation, some of these militant organizations split into smaller factions and groups. The relationship between KNO and KNF became strained after the Kuki-Naga conflict when both of them absorbed the cadres of Kuki Defence Force (KDF) in their respective areas of influence. While the killing of Mr. Thangkholun Haokip, the first Commander-in-Chief of KNO/KNA by its own cadres led to the formation of KNO/KNA Military Council, the killing of T. James Kuki by the KNF led to the formation of KNF Military Council (MC) with Mr. Seikam Kipgen as its president. However, the discontent brewing within the KNF (MC) finally boiled over, when a large number of its cadres broke away to form the Kuki Revolutionary Army (KRA) with K. Hangsing as its chief on December 15, 2000. Its proclaimed objective is to secure a separate Kuki State within the Union of India and reunification of the scattered Kukis in the State. Again, on March 29, 2000, the United Kuki Liberation Front (UKLF) was formed to fight for a separate State of the Kukis in North-East India. (Haokip 2010, 8)

Unification of Kuki Armed Groups

The first platform created to bring the unity of Kuki armed groups was the Indigenous People's Revolutionary Alliance (IPRA) with the initiative of KNO on May 27, 2000. The IPRA comprised of the ZRA (Zomi Revolutionary Army), Kuki National Army (KNA), Kuki National Front, Military Council (KNF-MC), Kuki National Front, President (KNF-P) and Hmar People's Democratic Council, Democratic (HPC-D). The objective of IPRA as stated by its leaders was to live together as an indigenous people without disturbing each other, although its main objective was to stop the infiltration of valley-based militants into their territory (Haokip 2010, 8). It, however, lasted only for a few years. In 2002, the Kuki National Council (KNC) was formed as an umbrella organization of the Kuki Revolutionary Army (KRA), Kuki National Front, Samuel (KNF-S) and United Kuki Liberation Front (UKLF). In 2006, KNF (P), KLA, HPC-D, KNF (S), ZRA and UKLF formed the United Peoples' Front (UPF) as a common platform at Aizawl to fulfil the ethnic aspirations of the Kuki-Chins. At present, the UPF comprises of Zomi Revolutionary Army, Kuki National Front (S), Kuki National Front (P), United Kuki Liberation Front, Kuki Revolutionary Army, Hmar People's Convention (D), and Kuki Liberation Army. The KNO's second attempt in bringing the various Kuki militant groups under its umbrella began in 2005, when KNF (MC) and KNF (Z) became its armed wings besides the KNA. In 2008, eleven armed groups became constituent armed wings of the Kuki National Organization (KNO). The armed wings of KNO are Kuki National Army, Kuki National Front (Military Council), Kuki National Front (Zogam), United Socialist Revolutionary Army, Hmar National Army, Zomi Revolutionary Front, United Komrem Revolutionary Army, United Minorities Liberation Front, Zou Defence Volunteer, Kuki Liberation Army, and Pakan Reunification Army (Haokip 2010, 8–9).

The regrouping of Kuki armed groups under KNO and UPF, which initially was largely based on threat perception of one group by another, is a significant development in the history of Kuki armed movement. With this, one main obstacle for forging unity has been resolved, as they have slowly stopped training their guns on each other. The leaders of Kuki armed groups seem to realise that the ideology of land and ethnic nationality is paramount over other local issues, which has led to the rejection of clan based politics.

Ideology

The political objectives of both KNO and UPF are identical in terms of the people represented and their territory. The only difference between the two is that while KNO demands statehood (one in India and another in Burma), the UPF demands one state in India. Both the UPF and KNO share the ideology of unifying the Kukis by adopting an inclusive Kuki identity based on its pre-British status and principles of federalism to ensure equal status of all constituents. Both the KNO and UPF argue that Kuki identity had existed in the pre-British period having sovereign authority over their land, arbitrarily divided by the British in the twentieth century. The Kukis fought against the British from 1917-1919 to protect their territory and again in 1943-1945 to regain their territory from the British (Haokip 2010, 8-9).

Suspension of Operation (SoO)

The Suspension of Operation (SoO) Agreement was signed between the Indian Army and Kuki armed groups in August 1, 2005. On August 22, 2008, the Kuki National Organization (KNO) and the United Peoples' Front (UPF) formally entered into tripartite agreement with the Central and Manipur State governments and signed the SoO to create conducive atmosphere for political dialogue (*Sangai Express* 2008, 1). This was indeed a positive measure for working out a tangible solution through peaceful means. In fact, this has been the desire and aspirations of the Kukis since the commencement of their movements in post-independence India.

However, at this stage, the relevant question is, would this be more effective than other ceasefire agreements that the Government of India has signed with other armed groups in North-East India? Will this serve to help the armed groups to reinforce their writ more openly and in a more brutal manner? Will it give the security forces the opportunity to divide the Kuki armed groups by playing off the weaker groups against the bigger ones and clandestinely instigating them to fight? The biggest challenge, however, is whether the signing of 'Suspension of Operation' (SoO) would lead to political dialogue to address and resolve the political problems of the Kukis. The apprehension of the Kuki people is that it would not usher in a peaceful solution. Such SoO or ceasefires, as seen in other parts of the region, have made little difference in terms of the de-escalation of violence or stepping up of the process of political settlement. Although SoO was supposed to be a transitory step towards final conflict resolution, it is on the threshold of becoming an end in itself providing some sort of legitimacy to the Kuki armed groups to carry on with their own agenda. The Manipur State and Central governments are more interested in using the Kuki armed groups to win elections rather than having political dialogues (Haokip 2010, 10).

The Kuki revolutionary groups on their part vehemently assert that the 'Kuki Nation' which has a distinct ethnic and socio-cultural identity has every right to self-determination, and that would be possible only when political autonomy (self-governance) is granted to them within the purview of the Constitution of India. The fulfilment of their aspirations is based on, "Article 244 and 244 (A) and Schedule I to IV of the Constitution of India", "...The tribals of North-Eastern India may or shall have separate administrative units for their own", and thus, the question is 'Why not Kukiland (Zalengam)'? (Kipgen, quoted in *Shillong Times*, October 1993)

Nevertheless, the Suspension of Operation (SoO) has opened up a new chapter in the annals of Kuki history. Emulating, John F. Kennedy's, "Let us never negotiate out of fear. Let us never fear to negotiate". The Kuki armed groups have signed the Suspension of Operations (SoO). "The purpose of signing the Suspension of Operation (SoO) with the Central and State governments is to hold a tripartite dialogue for a viable political settlement for the Kuki people, within the Constitution of India" (Haokip 2010, 9).

Conclusion

The Kuki National Assembly from its formative years did its best– struggling for the rights of the Kukis, by means of memorandums, petitions and prayers, having firm faith in the honesty and sincerity of the Government of free India. Keeping in mind that the higher authorities at the Centre understand well the history of the Kukis – a nation that once stood 'tooth and nail' against British imperialism. In pursuance of the long unfulfilled dreams of having a State for the Kuki people, a Committee christened as the Kuki State Demand Committee (KSDC), was formed in recent years that seeks a political solution for the Kuki people within the Constitution of India—the attainment of Kuki Statehood.

The KSDC following the footprints of the erstwhile KNA leaders pressurises the Government of India (GoI) so that the latter give a favourable response to the demands made by the Kukis in the sixties, for the establishment of a Kuki State. The KSDC has already sent a number of representations to the Government of India in this regard.

The future destiny of the Kuki Nation rests upon the outcome of the tripartite dialogue involving the Kuki UGs and the government at the Centre and at the State. Considering the recent positive development, such as outlining a road map for political dialogue, the Kuki people have reaffirmed their respect for democratic principles of the Constitution of India. Their efforts and interests have entered into a new stage. This is definitely a breakthrough. It is also hopeful that once the dialogue begins the Government of India will show its commitment and sincerity to democratic principles of rule of law and good governance.

REFERENCES

Baruah, Sanjib. (2005). *The Problem*. Paper presented at Gateway to the East: A Symposium on North East and the Look East Policy, June, in NEHU (North Eastern Hill University), Shillong, India.

Chaube, S.K. (1973). *Hill Politics in North-East India*. Calcutta: Orient Longman.

Gangte, T.S. (1993). *The Kukis of Manipur—A Historical Analysis*. New Delhi: Gyan Publishing House.

Haokip, T.T. (2010). *Kuki Armed Movements*. Sadar Hills District Level Kut Souvenir.

Haokip, Seilen. (2010). *Rhetorics of Kuki Nationalism—A Treatise*. New Delhi: Lustra Print.

Haokip, Thongkholal. (2010). Looking East *via* Moreh: Prospects and Challenges for the Kukis. In *Kuki Society: Past, Present and Future* edited by Ngamkhohao Haokip and Michael Lunminthang. New Delhi: Maxford Books.

Jeyaseelan, L. (1993). *Christianity and its Impacts: Socio-political and Economic.*

With Special Reference to Churachandpur District of Manipur. PhD Thesis, Manipur University.

Keivom, L. (2010). *Ethnic Nation Building Chin-Kuki-Zo Trail.* Paper presented at the Seminar organized by Kuki Research Forum and Sinlung Indigenous People's Human Rights Organisation (SIPHRO), Jawaharlal Nehru University Campus, 5th April, New Delhi, India.

Kipgen, Nehlun (1993). Founder of the KNF. *The Shillong Times*, 1st Oct and also in Ahsijolneng, Annual magazine, 2007, KSO Publication, Shillong Branch, 18-21.

Kipgen, Nehlun. (1993). Why not Kukiland for Kukis. *The Shillong Times*, October 1.

Maitra, Ramantanu and Susan Maitra. (1995). North-East India: The Target of British Apartheid. *Executive Intelligence Review*, 22(41), October.

Memorandum to the Prime Minister of India, Jawaharlal Nehru on 24/03/1960 vides the Kuki National Assembly (KNA) resolution adopted in its General Meeting at Thingkangphai, Churachandpur, from 19th to 22nd January, 1960.

Preamble to the Constitution of the Kuki National Assembly, North-East India, as amended at the General Assembly of the party held at Thingkangphai, Churachandpur, from19th-21st March, 1986.

Pudaite, Rosiem. (2002). *Indian National Struggle for Freedom and Its Impact on the Mizo Movement, 1935-1953.*

Ray, Asok Kumar. (1992). The Kuki National Assembly: Its Social Base and Working in Manipur. In *Regional Political Parties in North-East India*, edited by L.S. Gassah. Delhi: Omsons Publications.

Resolution of the Annual Kuki National Assembly Conference, 23rd to 25th October, 1946.

Resolution of the Kuki National Assembly, Working Committee, at Imphal, on the 16th May 1947.

Sharma, A. Basanta. (2003). *The Emergence and Working of Manipur People's Party (MPP) and Kuki National Assembly (KNA)—A Comparative Study.* PhD thesis, Manipur University.

S. Gangte, Thangkhomang. *Land Problem and Ethnic Tension in North-East India with Special Reference to Manipur.* A Monograph Cabinet nod to SoO deal. *The Sangai Express.* 23rd August, 2008.

Thomsong, Seikholen. (2005). Forgotten Sons: A Saga of Valour and Sacrifice. Unpublished Monograph.

Vaiphei, S. Prim. (1975). *The Vaiphei Tribe*. Imphal: MBC.

Vide. Election Commission of India, Notification No. 56/75-III, dated 14th April, 1975. See also the Constitution of the Kuki National Assembly, North-East India, p. 26.

Index